Best Egg Roll, Spring Roll, and Dumpling Recipes from Mama Li's Kitchen

Sarah Spencer

Editor: Marjorie Kramer
Marjorie.Kramer@aol.com

DISCLAIMER

All rights reserved. No part of this publication or the information in it may be quoted from or reproduced in any form by means such as printing, scanning, photocopying, or otherwise without prior written permission of the copyright holder.

Disclaimer and Terms of Use: Effort has been made to ensure that the information in this book is accurate and complete. However, the author and the publisher do not warrant the accuracy of the information, text, and graphics contained within the book due to the rapidly changing nature of science, research, known and unknown facts and internet. The Author and the publisher do not hold any responsibility for errors, omissions or contrary interpretation of the subject matter herein. This book is presented solely for motivational and informational purposes only.

CONTENTS

DISCLAIMER 2
CONTENTS 3
INTRODUCTION 1
COOKING ASIAN APPETIZERS 3
    FLAVORS 3
    ASIAN INGREDIENTS 4
    COOKING METHODS USED 5
    TOOLS NEEDED TO COOK ASIAN APPETIZERS 7
    DIFFERENCE BETWEEN EGG ROLLS AND SPRING ROLLS 9
COOKING TECHNIQUES 11
    FOLDING EGG ROLLS 12
    TWO MOST POPULAR WAYS TO FOLD EGG ROLLS. 13
    FOLDING SPRING ROLLS 13
    MAKING DUMPLINGS 23
    USING A BAMBOO STEAMER 25
EGG ROLL RECIPES 31
    EGG ROLL DOUGH RECIPE 31
    TRADITIONAL PORK EGG ROLLS 33
    DRAGON EGG ROLL 37
    VEGETABLE EGG ROLL 39
    ROAST PORK-STUFFED EGG ROLLS 41
    PO-PIA THOT (THAI) 43
    SHITAKE MUSHROOM AND TOFU EGG ROLL 47
    CHICKEN EGG ROLLS 51
    WATER CHESTNUT-SPECKLED EGG ROLLS 53
    SESAME CHICKEN EGG ROLL 55
    BEEF NOODLE EGG ROLLS 57
    SPICY CARROT EGG ROLLS 59
    MIXED EGG ROLL 61
    MUSHROOMS AND BEEF EGG ROLL 63
    TURON SABA *(FILIPINO DESSERT EGG ROLL)* 65
COLD SPRING ROLLS RECIPES 67
    VIETNAMESE FRESH SPRING ROLL 67

- Avocado and Mandarine Spring Rolls 69
- Roasted Pork Spring Rolls 71
- Peach Spring Rolls 73
- Asparagus Spring Roll 75
- Apple and Chicken Spring Rolls 77
- Ginger Chicken Spring Rolls 79
- Green Papaya Spring Rolls 81
- Rice Paper Recipe 83

FRIED AND BAKED SPRING ROLLS RECIPES 85

- Vietnamese Spring Roll 85
- Shrimp Spring Rolls 89
- Vegetable Lumpia 91
- Hoisin Chicken Spring Rolls 93
- Sesame Vegetable Spring Rolls 95
- Baked Pork Spring Rolls 99

DUMPLING RECIPES 103

- Dumpling Dough Recipes 103
- Pork and Shrimp Dumpling 105
- Pepper Pork Dumplings 107
- Beef and Caramelized Scallion Fried Dumplings 109
- Spicy Shrimp Dumplings 111
- Thai Trifecta Dumplings 113
- Mushroom Dumplings 115
- Curried Beef Dumplings 117
- Chicken and Leek Fried Dumplings 119
- Classic Chinese Dumplings 121
- Chicken Dumplings with Ginger-Coriander Dipping Sauce 125
- Shanghai Dumplings 127
- Mandu Dumplings (Korean dumplings) 131

DIM SUM FAVORITES 135

- Baked Pineapple Buns 136
- Steamed Barbeque Pork Buns 139
- Fried Taro Dumplings 142
- Seafood Dim Sum Dumplings 145

DIPPING SAUCES 147

- Quick & Easy Peanut Sauce 147

- Spicy Peanut Sauce 148
- Spicy Soy Dumpling Dipping Sauce 149
- Ginger Sauce 150
- Hoisin Dipping Sauce 151
- Honey Mustard Dipping Sauce 152
- Classic Soy and Vinegar Dipping Sauce for Dumplings 153
- Classic Plum Sauce 154
- Quick and Easy Orange Dipping Sauce 156
- Sweet and Sour Dipping Sauce 157
- Sweet and Hot Dipping Sauce 158
- Hot Chili Sauce 159
- Honey Ginger Sauce 160
- Caramel Dipping Sauce for Turon 161

BONUS RECIPES 163
- Shrimp Toasts 163
- Crispy Fried Wontons 165
- Shrimp Balls 167
- Kon Tiki Bobo Meatballs 169
- Tanguy BBQ Pork Short Ribs – Chinese style 171

CONCLUSION 173
ABOUT THE AUTHOR 175
APPENDIX 178
- Cooking Conversion Charts 178

INTRODUCTION

Mama Li came to America, all the way from China, when she was just 13 years old. She met her husband while working in the kitchen of a New York City Chinatown restaurant. Eventually, they had five children and moved to the Philadelphia area where, as husband and wife, they operated a Chinese takeout restaurant. I became friends with her youngest daughter, Jade, who went to the same school as me. We quickly became best friends. I used to visit the restaurant often after school with Jade. We would watch Mama Li prepare the orders. When I got older, Mama Li gave me my first summer job, cooking in her kitchen. What an experience it was! Hot, fast, exhausting, but also rewarding! I learned to cook well and prepare mouth-watering Asian food with only one pan, the wok. I still have the old, beat up wok she gave me when my family moved to Canada a few years later.

In this book, you will find the best egg rolls, spring rolls, and dumplings recipes I learned from Mama Li and her wonderful family. I have adapted the recipes over the years to fit my own family's diet requirements and taste.

Having the whole family participate can make your meal preparation much more enjoyable. You'll need good supervision of the little ones since there is chopping involved. Everyone has specific instructions to cut up the vegetables and other ingredients.

I hope you will enjoy making these appetizers recipes.

Sarah

COOKING ASIAN APPETIZERS

Flavors

Asian cooking is all about flavors. The spices and condiments used in Asian cooking are aromatic and taste delightful. By aromatic, I mean an incredible, appetizing smell that floods your senses.

Asian cooking is completely based on fresh ingredients. It avoids canned foods and thus, the food rates very high on health scales. People in the most parts of Asia prefer to put organic ingredients in their food, be it vegetables or meat. Asian food is like a party for all your senses, but especially the taste buds!

When cooking the Asian food, a pantry full of all the essentials will help to get the taste right. Other than spices, there are a lot of other "must-haves," like flour, coconut, and vegetables. In the Asian category, you will find a plethora of options in both vegetarian as well as non-vegetarian food.

Be it meat, sea food, or breads, Asia does everything differently. In this book, you will learn and taste the awesomeness of Asian cooking. There are hundreds of recipes that go back thousands of years, and have been equally loved by all generations.

Cooking in Asia is an important part of the daily routine. Men and women spend a lot of time in their kitchens, giving the routine cooking a personal touch. Asian food is varied. You will find many different types of food on the menu. There are soups, curries, salads, bread, noodles, finger foods, and many more options that you can choose.

Asian Ingredients

To cook Asian foods, you will need to stock on certain ingredients. These include:

1. Soya sauce
2. Fish Sauce
3. Oyster Sauce
4. Curry Paste
5. Rice Vinegar
6. Chili Sauce
7. Miso Paste
8. Coconut Milk
9. Cloves
10. Garlic
11. Red pepper

12. Sugar
13. Ginger
14. Garlic
15. Lime
16. Cilantro
17. Rice noodles
18. RIce
19. All-purpose flour
20. Wine
21. Sesame Oil
22. Olive Oil
23. Grape seed oil

Cooking Methods Used

Asian Cooking includes a lot of techniques. Some of which are:

1. Steaming

Asian food boasts of a lot of recipes that can be steamed. This leads to minimum usage of oil, making it a very healthy diet. You will either use a bamboo steamer or a double boiler.

2. Boiling

Many other dishes are boiled, again giving a lot of nutritional value to the food. Boiling ensures that the nutrients of the food are not lost in the cooking process (as they use the stock or broth used for boiling in the actual cooking process).

3. Frying

Frying is a very important method in Asian cooking. A lot of dishes are best eaten when fried and crispy. Some of which are wontons, dumplings, and noodles, which are the yummiest when fried. A wok works best, but you can also use a large deep skillet.

4. Roasting

Roasting forms the backbone of the Asian cooking. A lot of dishes taste best when roasted. Tofu, pork, chicken, and many more make for some delicious roasted dishes.

5. Baking

Baking is a very healthy way of cooking. This method ensures a minimum requirement of oil. A lot of Chinese and other Asian dishes are so versatile that they can be baked instead of frying them, giving Asian cooking a very healthy twist.

Cooking in Asia is a very healthy process. A lot of stress is laid on preserving the nutrients in the food. People in

Asian countries believe there has to be a balance in cooking, be it in taste or colors. They believe that balance brings good Chi to the food, which in turn benefits the body and mind in multiple ways.

Asia is a huge continent and has a wide variety of food styles. Each area has its own authentic methods. It goes without saying that each region picks up cooking styles from other neighboring regions. Because of this you will easily find traces and tastes of one cuisine in another.

Asian cooking tends to be on the hot side, with liberal uses of many different spices and chilies. Western food is usually bland by comparison. Many Westerners can get a bit of a surprise when it comes to the taste of Asian food.

Tools Needed to Cook Asian Appetizers

If you plan to include Asian food in your house hold meals, you should have at least some of the following:

1. A steam cooker
2. A wok or a very large frying pan
3. A boiler/container with a strainer
4. Baking trays
5. Bamboo steamer

Once you have stocked these in your kitchen, you can whip up any of the dishes mentioned in this book and have an Asian cuisine theme party anytime! The recipes presented in this book are very simple to make and are sure to bring you accolades galore. Have a good time cooking the best Asian rolls and dumplings recipes!

Difference between Egg Rolls and Spring Rolls

Egg rolls have a thicker and more chewy dough.

Fried spring rolls are made with a thin rice flour dough that is light and crispy.

Originally, egg rolls originated in China whereas Spring Rolls came from Viet Nam.

Egg rolls are usually wrapped in thicker, egg-based dough and are fried or baked, while Spring rolls are wrapped in thinner, rice flour-based dough. The filling differs from one country to another, and everyone has their own version of egg rolls and spring rolls. Both can come meatless. Spring rolls can be served cold or hot. When they are not cooked, they are sometimes called summer rolls or garden rolls. They also differ in sizes. Served as an appetizer, an egg roll will be a bit smaller than a Spring roll, whereas served as a main dish, egg rolls tend to be larger.

Cold spring rolls. Fresh and cooked ingredients are layered in a rice paper wrapper.

COOKING TECHNIQUES

Here are a series of pictures showing the techniques to help you prepare any Asian appetizer and detailed instructions for each technique. It includes folding, spring rolls, making dumplings, and steaming dumplings using a bamboo steamer. Although each recipe does indicate how to do it, it's always nice to have an image to refer to. The egg rolls and spring rolls can be folded using the same technique.

The techniques are quite simple once you get a hang of it. The egg rolls and spring rolls will be more tightly wrapped and easier to make as you get more and more practice.

One tip to make it easier when making egg rolls, dumplings, and spring rolls is to prepare a clean working surface when you are ready to roll and fold. Have your fillings, all the ingredients, and the dough wrappers you need within arm's reach of your working surface. Also, prepare a sealing liquid that will act as glue to seal. You can either use a small bowl of water or some egg wash. Egg wash is made with an egg and one or two tablespoons of water. Whisk the egg wash well before using.

Folding Egg Rolls

Folding is really easy. The trick is not to overload your egg roll with too much filling. Otherwise, it will be more difficult to roll it. Egg roll wrappers are available in most supermarkets in the Asian frozen food section or at any Asian market (fresh or frozen). They come mainly in two sizes: small and large. You can use either one. Thaw the dough completely before using. It will be easier to separate the wrappers.

Place a wrapper on a clean, dry, working surface. Spoon some filling in a straight line in the middle of the first half, leaving enough space to fold on the sides and the bottom. For large wrappers, leave about 1 ½ inches on the sides and about 2 inches on the bottom. For the smaller wrappers, leave about ¾ inches on the sides and about one inch on the bottom.

Fold the bottom over the filling. Brush the top of the wrapper lightly and the edge of the inside of the sides with water or egg wash to seal your egg roll. Roll completely and press slightly on the seam to seal it as well as both sides. Place the prepared egg rolls on a plate. They are now ready to be fried or baked. You can also fold them like spring rolls.

Two most popular ways to fold egg rolls.

Folding Spring Rolls

Spring rolls with rice paper (cold rolls)

Rice paper wrappers are available in most supermarkets in the Asian food isle or at any Asian market.

The first thing to do is to prepare a large enough dish to place a rice paper in. Fill it with lukewarm water. Dip the rice paper in completely for a few seconds. It will become very soft. Delicately remove it from the water, and place it flat on your working surface.

Place a leaf of lettuce on the rice paper if your recipe asks for it. Next, layer your ingredients, or spoon some of the filling in so that all your ingredients lie in a straight line above the center of the rice paper middle, leaving yourself enough space to fold on top and on each side; about 2 inches on top and about 1 inch on the sides.

To fold, start by folding both sides toward the center and then do the top part. Roll the spring roll tightly. Since the dough is wet, it will stick together easily.

Once rolled tightly, place it on a serving plate. Cover with a plastic wrap to keep them moist. You can also wrap each roll individually.

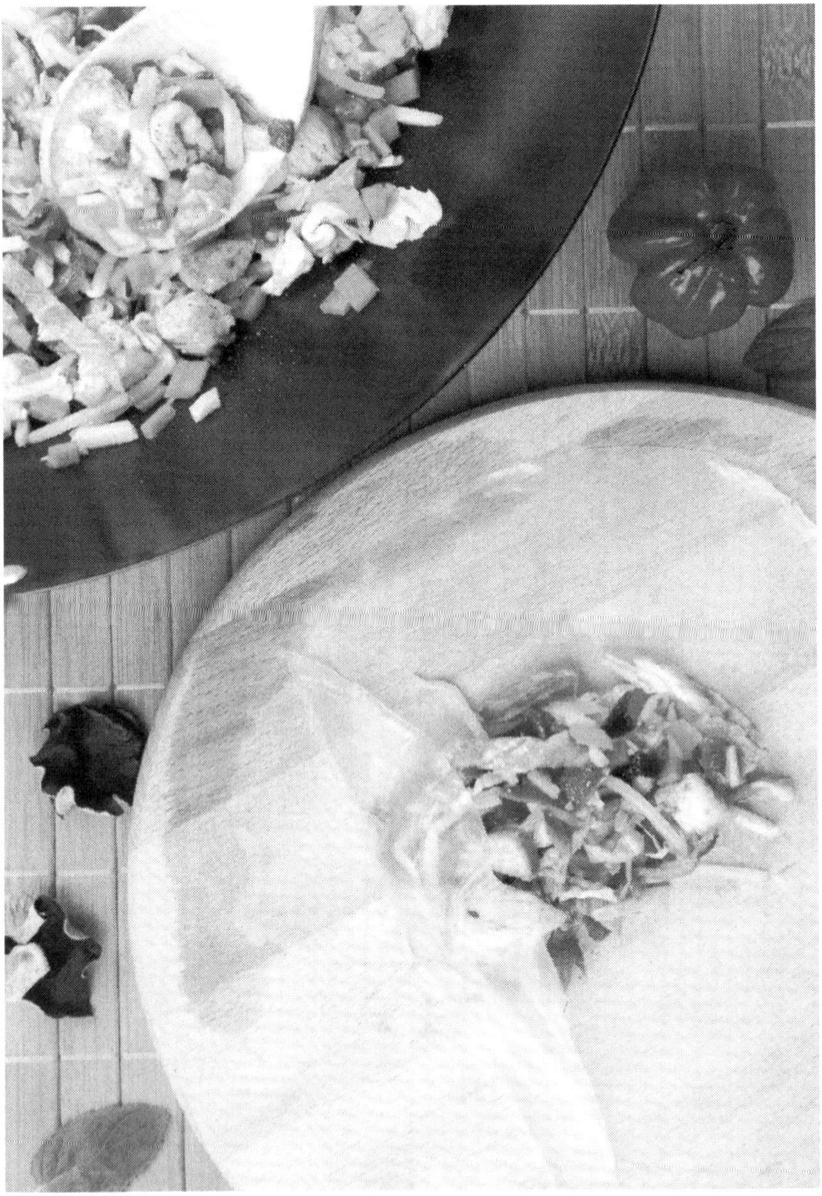

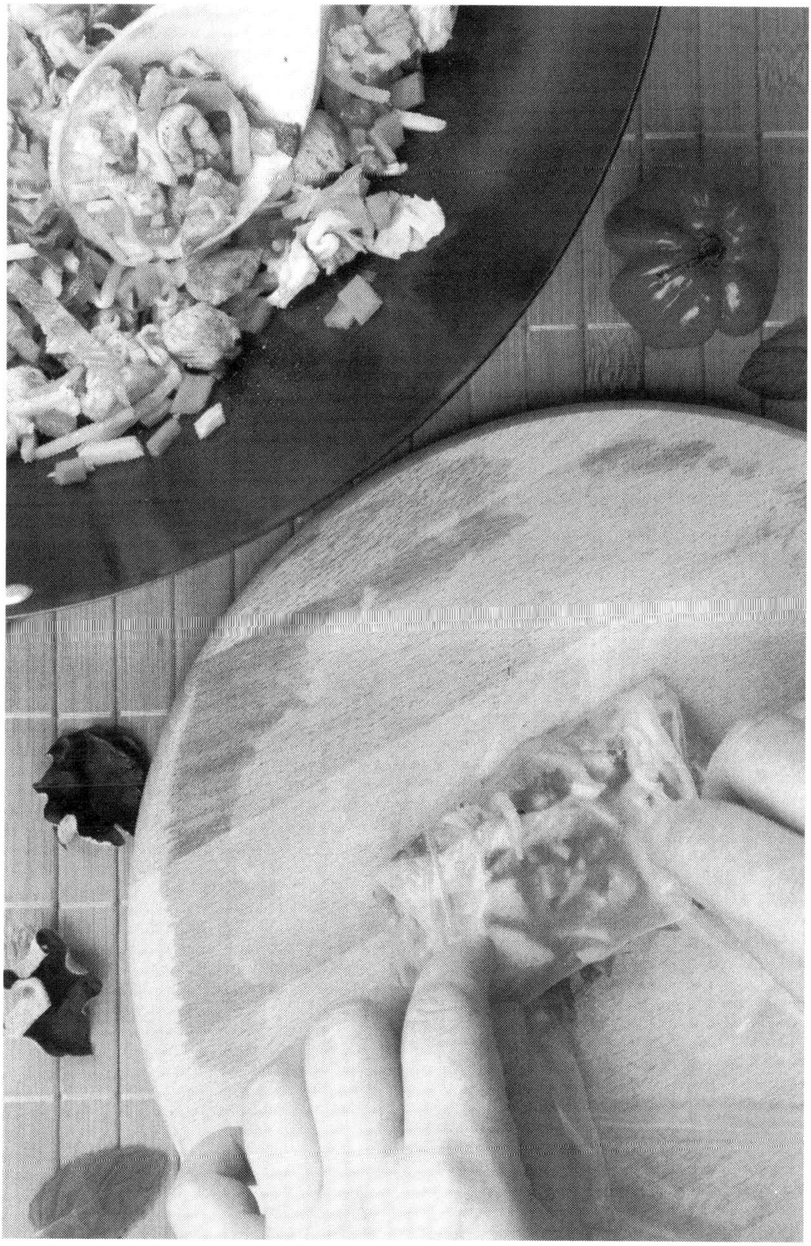

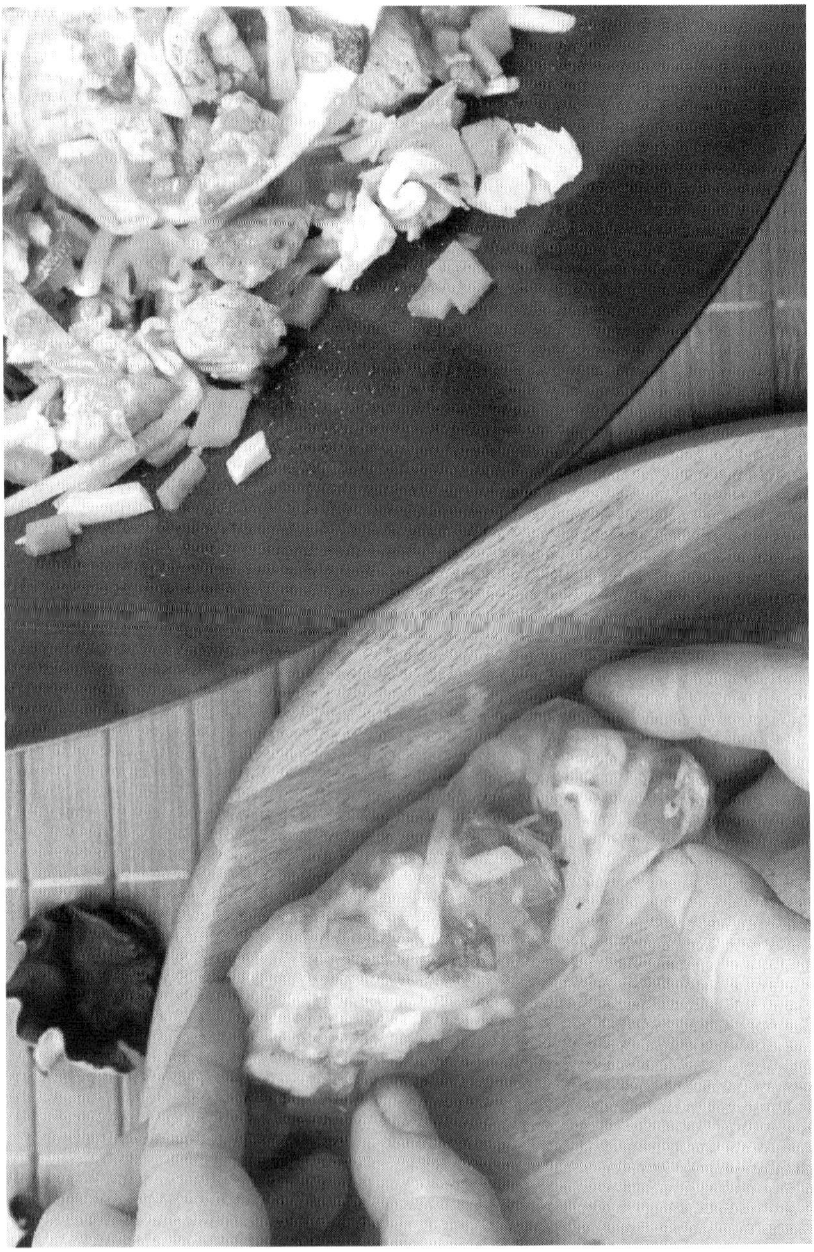

With dough (fried or baked spring rolls)

It's basically the same technique, but you will need a liquid like an egg wash to seal the spring roll dough together. The spring roll wrappers that you can get from an Asian market or in the grocery store are generally sold in two sizes and shapes: small and large, round and square. I like to use the larger square ones as they are less time consuming and easier to roll. If you are making your own dough, you can decide on the size that you want.

I like to place the filling on a diagonal line in the middle of the wrapper, leaving enough space on each side to fold, about 1½ inch on each side. Try not to overload the roll with too much filling.

To wrap, just fold both sides on top of the filling. Bring one of the pointy tops over the filling and roll till you reach the other pointy top.

Finally, once the sides and bottom are folded, gently brush some water on the edges of the upper triangle with water or egg wash (whisk together one egg with 1-2 tablespoons of cold water). Roll and seal the spring roll.

Place the rolls on a plate. They are now ready to be baked or fried.

Making Dumplings

Dumplings come in all shapes and sizes. Typically, you will be using a round dough wrapper. They can be folded in many ways. The simplest way is to place the filling on in the middle of the dumpling and fold over to form a half moon shape. To seal the dumpling, lightly brush some water or egg wash on the edges of the dough. Lightly press down to seal the dumpling. You can also pleat it by pinching the dough over at even intervals.

Here is a series of pictures showing the whole process of making dumplings from scratch.

There are many more techniques for folding your dumplings. One I like to use is placing the filling in the middle of the larger round wrapper and sealing with water or egg wash on top of the filling. And making some pleats at regular intervals.

Using a Bamboo Steamer

Dumplings, once prepared, need to be steamed. In traditional Chinese cuisine, you will steam your dumpling in a bamboo steamer. I highly recommend that you get this cooking tool as it will become your best friend not only to steam dumplings, but also many other foods such as vegetables, meat, fish, and seafood. It is one of the healthiest ways to prepare food. It retains all the good nutrients and vitamins of the food you eat while infusing all the flavors you want to each ingredient.

A bamboo steamer is made of several tiers so you can cook different food simultaneously. They come in different sizes, and you can choose which one is more appropriate for your needs. The maintenance is also very easy. You just need to wash it lightly with hot water and a gentle soap. Make sure to let it dry thoroughly to prevent premature wear or mold formation.

You can get a bamboo steamer in Asian markets, specialized cooking stores, and even online. Depending on how many tiers you want, it will probably cost you less than $20 for a good one.

To create the steam and cook your food, the bamboo steamer will need to be placed on simmering water. You can use any pot from a large skillet to a wok or even a stock pot. To prevent burning, make sure that the sides of the steamer do not touch the side of your pot. Also ensure that the water does not touch the food. I like to use the wok because it sits just above the simmering water and the sides are unconstrained.

The cooking technique is quite simple once you have the proper tools. If you are using a large skillet, place it over medium-high heat with 2 inches of water. Bring the water to a boil. Lower the heat to medium so that you keep an intense simmering of the water.

Place large lettuce leaf or cabbage leaves at the bottom of each tier where you will be placing your food. This is to prevent it from sticking to the bottom. You can also use parchment paper that you cut in a circle to fit the bottom and pierce with a few holes to let the steam go through. If you would like to infuse more flavor to your food, you could also use banana leaves or corn leaves.

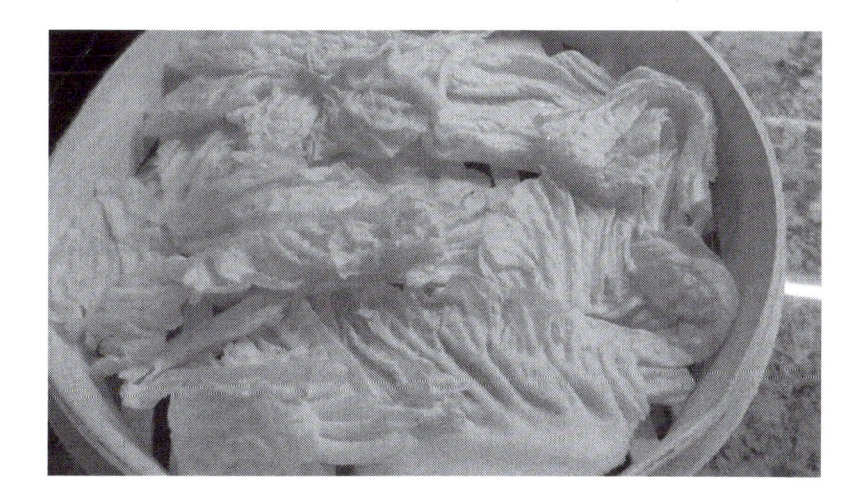

Place the dumplings in one row with enough space between them so they do not touch each other. This will prevent them from sticking to one another after they are cooked.

Place your bamboo steamer with its cover tightly on over the simmering water. The food will start to warm up and steam after just a few minutes. Typically, it will take between 15 and 20 minutes to cook dumplings with meat in them, and a bit less for vegetable-only dumplings. Don't forget to add water as needed if it starts to evaporate too quickly. The bottom should remain well covered. Check the progression of the cooking process a few times.

Note: I use this old wok only for steaming. The water should be simmering when you place tour bamboo steamer in it. Make sure the water does not touch the food in the lowest tier. You can also use a deep skillet or large enough saucepan.

Once the dumplings are cooked through, remove the bamboo steamer with potholder gloves to protect your hands from the hot steam. Be careful for your face also. Use tongs and gloves to remove the hot dumplings to place them on a service plate with your favorite dipping sauces.

You can prepare your dumplings a day ahead and place them in an airtight container in the refrigerator. You can either steam them again for 4-6 minutes or pan-fry them.

If you like your dumplings to be crispy, warm up some oil in a frying pan over medium-high heat and pan-fry the dumplings on all sides until golden brown. It should take only a few minutes.

Note: you can freeze dumplings easily. Just place them in airtight containers or sealable freezer bags before steaming them. It's a good idea to sprinkle a little flour over your dumplings so they do not stick together and are dry when you freeze them. To cook, make sure to thaw the dumplings completely and steam as indicated above.

EGG ROLL RECIPES

Here, you will learn about different Asian techniques to make traditional egg rolls.

Egg Roll Dough Recipe

Have you always wanted to make your own egg roll wraps? Here's a perfect recipe to make wraps. Making these on your own ensures that your egg roll recipe is completely homemade and free of any preservatives or unwanted ingredients.

Yields: 10
Preparation time: 60 minutes
Cooking time: none

Ingredients:
1 large egg, beaten
2 cups flour
1 teaspoon salt
½ cup cold water

Preparation:
1. In a dry bowl, mix the flour and the salt.

2. To it, add the egg and cold water, to make a dough.
3. Knead the dough to make it very smooth and elastic.
4. Wrap the dough in a plastic wrap, and refrigerate for 20-30 minutes.
5. Break the dough into 16 even pieces.
6. Roll them finely into squares using a rolling pin.
7. Make sure that wraps are extremely thin.
8. Keep them covered with a damp kitchen towel or plastic wrap to avoid drying until the wrap is completed.
9. Your egg roll wraps are ready to go.

Traditional Pork Egg Rolls

This is one of the most Classic Chinese egg rolls. It is a balanced mix of ground pork and vegetables. It is a tasty appetizer and a must-have for pork lovers.

Serves: 10 pieces
Preparation time:
Cooking time: 30 minutes

Ingredients:

10 spring egg roll wrappers
1 tablespoon cornstarch mixed in water to seal the egg rolls
Oil for frying

Pork mix ingredients
½ pound ground pork
Freshly ground black pepper
½ tablespoon soya sauce
½ teaspoon cornstarch
¼ teaspoon white sugar

Vegetable mix ingredients
2 garlic cloves, very finely minced
1 carrot, shredded, medium-sized
¼ head of green cabbage, shredded

5 shiitake mushrooms

1 teaspoon fresh ginger, grated

1 teaspoon Chinese rice wine

1 teaspoon soya sauce

2 tablespoons grape seed oil, separated

2 teaspoons rice wine

2-3 teaspoons soya sauce

¼ teaspoon sugar

Salt and black Pepper

1 teaspoon sesame oil

Preparation:

1. Begin the preparation by marinating the filling. In a mixing bowl, combine all the ingredients for the ground pork, and let it marinate for 10 minutes.
2. Grate the vegetables and the mushrooms.
3. Coat a wok or a large frying pan with the grape seed oil on medium-high heat. Add the pork, and fry till the color changes. Remove the pork from the wok to a plate and set aside.
4. Add grape seed oil and the vegetables to the wok. Begin with ginger and garlic, and follow with vegetables, stirring constantly.
5. Once everything is fried and soft, add the sesame oil, rice wine, soya sauce, sugar, and black pepper. Cook for one minute on low heat.

6. Finally, add the pork back in and mix everything. Cook for another minute.
7. Remove from heat, and let it cool.
8. Try and remove the extra moisture with paper towels.
9. Spread the egg wraps on a flat surface. Fill each of them with one tablespoon of the filling.
10. Roll and seal them perfectly using the water and corn starch mixture. For the rolling method for egg rolls, turn to page 12.
11. Once done, cover the egg rolls with a clean, wet towel so that they do not dry.
12. Refrigerate for 4 hours before frying them in oil.

Dragon Egg Roll

Serves: 12 pieces
Preparation time: 15 minutes
Cooking time: 15 minutes

Ingredients:

12 large egg roll wraps

½ to 1 pound ground chicken

2 teaspoons freshly grated ginger

½ or 1 hot peppers such as small Chinese Chi-Chien hot peppers or Thai hot peppers, minced finely

2 garlic cloves, minced

1 teaspoon sugar

1 teaspoon salt

1 teaspoon sesame oil

¼ cup soya sauce

16-ounce bag shredded cabbage

1 carrot, shredded

4 green onions, finely chopped

1 egg, beaten with 1 tablespoon of water

Oil (for frying)

Preparation:

1. In a wok, set to medium-high heat, stir-fry the ground chicken with ginger, hot peppers and garlic.

2. Follow with sugar, salt, sesame oil, and soya sauce.
3. Add the vegetables in. Stir-fry for 1-2 minutes more and remove from heat.
4. Let the mixture cool.
5. Set the wrappers on a flat surface. Fill each one of them using 2-3 tablespoons of the mixture.
6. Roll/fold the egg rolls and seal using the beaten egg. For the complete egg roll folding technique, turn to page 12.
7. Place the prepared eggrolls in a plate and refrigerate covered with a plastic wrap until ready to fry.
8. Heat the oil in a frying pan to 350°F/177°C.
9. Fry each of the eggrolls for 1 to 2 minutes on each side until golden brown.
10. Place egg rolls on plate lined with paper towels to catch any excess oil before serving.

Vegetable Egg Roll

Serves: 10 pieces
Preparation: 20 minutes
Cooking time: 20 minutes

Ingredients:

3 cup shredded cabbage

1 cup broccoli florets, chopped

1 cup soya bean sprout

⅓ cup snow peas or sugar snap peas, sliced

⅓ cup shredded carrot

⅓ cup green onions, sliced (a.k.a. scallions)

2 tablespoons vegetable oil

1 teaspoon fresh ginger, grated

1 garlic clove, minced

1 tablespoon rice vinegar

1 tablespoon sesame oil

1 tablespoon reduced sodium soya sauce

1 pinch red pepper flakes, crushed (more if you like it very spicy)

10 egg roll wrappers

1 egg beaten with 1 tablespoon of water

Preparation:

1. In a large bowl, mix all the vegetables except the green onions.

2. Heat a wok or a large frying pan with 2 tablespoons of vegetable oil.
3. Add garlic, green onions, and ginger, and fry 30 seconds to 1 minute, until slightly golden and fragrant.
4. Add in the vegetable mixture. Stir-fry for a few minutes until the vegetables are tender. Stir in the soya sauce, rice vinegar and red pepper flakes. Cook for another minute until all ingredients are well combined.
5. Take the mixture off the heat, and let it cool.
6. In the meantime, prepare your eggroll wrappers on a clean working surface and the egg wash.
7. Fill the wrappers with 2-3 tablespoons of the vegetable mixture and roll tightly. For the egg roll folding technique, turn to page 12.
8. Heat the oil in a frying pan to 350°F/177°C.
9. Fry each of the eggrolls for 1 to 2 minutes on each side until golden brown. Let rest on paper towels to absorb excess fat
10. You can also bake these eggrolls. Pre-heat the oven to 375°F/191°C. Brush each eggroll with vegetable oil. Place them on the baking tray lined with parchment paper. Bake for 10 minutes on both sides, until golden. Serve warm with dipping sauce. like an orange dipping sauce or plum sauce.

Roast Pork-Stuffed Egg Rolls

Serves: 18
Preparation time: 15 minutes
Cooking time: 30 minutes

Ingredients:

½ pound cooked roast pork

1 celery stalk, finely diced

2 carrots, shredded

2 green onions, minced

1 tablespoon fresh ginger, grated

2 cloves garlic, minced

3 tablespoons low-sodium soy sauce

1 tablespoon oyster sauce

1 egg beaten with 1 tablespoon of water

Extra light olive oil for frying

18 small egg roll wrappers

Preparation:

1. Slice roast pork into ¼" strips.
2. Combine pork with celery stalk, carrots, green onions, ginger, garlic, soy sauce, oyster sauce and marinate for 10 minutes.
3. Set your wrapper on flat surface with one corner pointed at you.

4. Place 1 to 1½ tablespoons of filling on the bottom of the wrapper, about two inches above the corner point.
5. Fold the bottom part of the wrapper over the filling, and then fold the sides over the filling – so you have what almost looks like an envelope with a long flap.
13. Roll away from you until you get about two inches from the top, brush the edges at the top with your egg wash, complete roll and repeat. For the complete folding method for egg rolls, turn to page 12.
6. Once you have all of your rolls set, line a plate with paper towels.
7. Fill a heavy frying pot or use a wok, halfway up with oil, deep fry egg rolls until golden brown, about 1-2 minutes on each side. You can also use a deep frying machine.
8. Place egg rolls on plate with paper towels to catch any excess oil before serving.
9. Serve warm with your favorite dipping sauce.

Po-Pia Thot (Thai)

Serves: 18
Preparation time: 20 minutes
Cooking time: 20 minutes

Ingredients:

1 pound ground pork

4 dried tree ear mushrooms

1 cup Glass noodles

1 small onion, diced

½ cup mung beans

4 cloves garlic, minced

¼ cup low-sodium soy sauce

1 egg

4 tablespoons extra light olive oil

18 egg roll wrappers

Preparation:

1. Place Glass noodles and dried tree ear mushrooms in a bowl of warm water to soak.
2. Fill a large pot with water and bring to rolling boil over medium-high heat.
3. Whisk egg, set aside.
4. Divide up your pork into small pieces – roughly 1½" - add to the boiling water, and cook for a 2-4 minutes, drain and place in a large bowl.

5. Drain Glass noodles and mushrooms, give them a rough chop so noodles are shorter in length.
6. Add to bowl along with onion, mung beans, garlic, and soy sauce.
7. Heat 4 tablespoons olive oil in a wok. Add meat and veggies, sauté for two minutes.
8. Add egg into the middle of the wok, scramble, and combine with meat and veggies. Remove from heat.
9. Set your wrapper on flat surface with one corner pointed at you.
10. Place a tablespoon of filling on the bottom of the wrapper, about two inches above the corner point.
11. Fold the bottom part of the wrapper over the filling, and then fold the sides over the filling so you have what almost looks like an envelope with a long flap.
12. Roll the spring roll away from you until you get about two inches from the top, brush the edges at the top with your egg wash, complete roll and repeat.
13. Once you have all of your rolls set, line a plate with paper towels.
14. Pour frying oil in a heavy pot or a wok and fill halfway up. Deep fry egg rolls until golden brown, about 1 to 2 minutes on both sides.

15. Place egg rolls on plate with paper towels to catch any excess oil before serving.
16. Serve with your favorite dipping sauce like a spicy peanut sauce or a chili sauce.

Shitake Mushroom and Tofu Egg Roll

Serves: 18
Preparation time: 15 minutes
Cooking time: 15 minutes

Ingredients:

½ pound tofu

8 Shitake Mushrooms

1 celery stalk, finely-diced

2 carrots, shredded

2 green onions, minced

1 clove garlic, minced

3 tablespoons low-sodium soy sauce

1 tablespoon oyster sauce

1 egg

¼ cup extra light olive oil

18 egg roll wrappers

Oil for frying

Preparation:

1. Slice roasted tofu into ½" pieces.
2. Heat ¼ cup extra virgin olive oil in wok over medium heat.
3. Stir-fry tofu until golden brown, remove from wok, and set aside.

4. Rough chop Shitake mushrooms and combine with celery, carrots, green onions, garlic and soy sauce.
5. Add mushroom mixture to the wok, and stir-fry for 2-3 minutes until vegetables are tender. Add the tofu to the vegetable mix. Remove from heat, and cool down for 10 minutes.
6. Set your wrappers on flat surface with one corner pointed at you.
7. Place a tablespoon of filling on the bottom of the wrapper, about two inches above the corner point.
8. Fold the bottom part of the wrapper over the filling, and then fold the sides over the filling – so you have what almost looks like an envelope with a long flap.
9. Roll the spring roll away from you until you get about two inches from the top, brush the edges at the top with your egg wash, complete roll and repeat.
10. Once you have all of your rolls set, line a plate with paper towels.
11. Fill a heavy frying pot or a wok halfway up with oil, deep fry egg rolls until golden brown, about 1-2 minutes on each sides. You can also use a deep frying machine.

12. Place egg rolls on plate with paper towels to catch any excess oil before serving.
13. Serve with your favorite dipping sauce like the Sweet'n Hot Pineapple Dipping Sauce.

Chicken Egg Rolls

Serves: 12
Preparation time: 15 minutes
Cooking time: 15 minutes

Ingredients:

1 pound ground chicken

4 tablespoons extra light olive oil

2 tablespoons fresh ginger, grated

1 cup cabbage, shredded

1 carrot, shredded

¼ cup low-sodium soy sauce

1 tablespoon flour

2 tablespoons water

12 egg roll wrappers

Vegetable oil for frying

Preparation:

1. Mix water, flour, set aside.
2. Heat 4 tablespoons of extra virgin olive oil in a skillet over medium heat.
3. Add ground chicken, brown, remove from heat.
4. Mix in ginger, cabbage, carrots, and soy sauce.
5. Place egg roll wrapper on a flat surface with one corner pointed at you.

6. Place one heaping tablespoon of filling about three inches above bottom corner. Roll bottom corner over wrapper and fold over the left side and then the right side over the wrapper, continue to roll up to one inch below the top corner, brush the top edges with water and flour mixture and seal wrapper. Repeat for next roll.
7. Fill a heavy frying pot or wok with vegetable oil. Bring the oil temperature to 350°F/177°F. Fry the egg rolls in small batches until golden brown, about 1 to 2 minutes per side. You can also use a deep frying machine.
8. Place the eggrolls on a plate lined with kitchen paper towels to drain the excess fat.
9. Serve hot with your favorite dipping sauce.

Water Chestnut-Speckled Egg Rolls

Serves: 12

Preparation time: 15 minutes

Cooking time: 30 minutes

Ingredients:

1 cup water chestnuts, chopped

2 green onions, chopped

8 baby corn, quartered

1 cup cooked mung beans

1 cup green cabbage, shredded

¼ cup soy sauce

1 teaspoon black pepper

1 tablespoon rice wine vinegar

1 egg

Extra light olive oil

12 egg roll wrappers

Preparation:

1. Combine black pepper, rice wine vinegar, and soy sauce in a bowl.
2. In a second bowl combine green onions, baby corn, water chestnuts, mung beans, and green cabbage, add the soy sauce mixture, and allow to sit for 20 minutes.

3. Place egg roll wrapper on a flat surface with one corner pointed at you.
4. Place one heaping tablespoon of filling about three inches above bottom corner, roll bottom corner over wrapper and fold over the left side and then the right side over the wrapper. Continue to roll up to one inch below the top corner, brush the top edges with water and flour mixture and seal wrapper, repeat.
5. Fill a heavy frying pot halfway with oil or you can also fry the eggrolls in a wok. Let the oil reach 350°F/177°F. Deep fry egg rolls until golden brown, about 1-2 minute per side. You can also use a deep frying machine.
6. Place egg rolls on plate lined with paper towels to catch any excess oil before serving.
7. Serve with your favorite dipping sauce.

Sesame Chicken Egg Roll

Serves: 12

Preparation time: 40 minutes

Cooking time: 20 minutes

Ingredients:

1 pound chicken breast

2 tablespoons ginger grated

1 carrot, shredded

1 red bell pepper, seeded, julienned

¼ cup low-sodium soy sauce

2 tablespoons sesame paste

¼ cup sesame seeds

4 tablespoons extra light olive oil

12 egg roll wrappers

Oil for frying

Preparation:

1. Mix water, flour, set aside.
2. Slice chicken breasts into ½" cubes.
3. Heat 2 tablespoons of extra virgin olive oil in a large skillet or a wok over medium heat.
4. Add chicken, sauté until browned. Set the meat on a plate to rest. Drain the excess fat. With paper towels.

5. Add 1 or 2 tablespoons of olive oil to the pan. Stir-fry the ginger, carrot, red bell pepper until the vegetables are tender, about 3 minutes. Stir-in soy sauce, sesame paste and sesame seeds. Remove from heat.
6. Add the chicken back in the vegetable mix and stir until well combined.
7. Place egg roll wrapper on a flat surface with one corner pointed at you.
8. Place one heaping tablespoon of filling about three inches above bottom corner, roll bottom corner over wrapper and fold over the left side and then the right side over the wrapper, continue to roll up to one inch below the top corner, brush the top edges with water and flour mixture and seal wrapper, repeat.
9. Fill a heavy frying pot halfway with oil or you can also fry the eggrolls in a wok. Let the oil reach 350°F/177°C. Deep fry egg rolls until golden brown, about 1-2 minute per side. You can also use a deep frying machine.
10. Place egg rolls on plate lined with paper towels to catch any excess oil before serving.
11. Serve with your favorite dipping sauce.

Beef Noodle Egg Rolls

Serves: 12
Preparation time: 20 minutes
Cooking time: 30 minutes

Ingredients:

1 pound ground beef
½ cup dry Chow Mein noodles
2 celery stalks, finely chopped
3 cloves garlic, minced
2 tablespoons fresh ginger, grated
1 cup cabbage, shredded
2 green onions, chopped
3 tablespoons soy sauce
1 tablespoon Hoisin sauce
1 teaspoon black pepper
Extra light olive oil
12 egg roll wrappers

Preparation:

1. Soak Chow Mein in warm water.
2. Heat 4 tablespoons of extra virgin olive oil in a skillet over medium heat.
3. Add garlic and onion, and stir-fry for 30 seconds to a minute until tender and fragrant. Add ground beef, brown, and remove from heat.

4. Add cabbage, Chow Mein noodles, and ginger to skillet along with hoisin sauce, pepper, and soy sauce.
5. Place egg roll wrapper on a flat surface with one corner pointed at you.
6. Place one heaping tablespoon of filling about three inches above bottom corner, roll bottom corner over wrapper and fold over the left side and then the right side over the wrapper, continue to roll up to one inch below the top corner, brush the top edges with water and flour mixture and seal wrapper, repeat.
7. Fill a heavy frying pot halfway with oil, or you can also fry the eggrolls in a wok. Let the oil reach 350°F//177°F. Deep fry egg rolls until golden brown, about 1-2 minutes per side. You can also use a deep frying machine.
8. Place egg rolls on plate lined with paper towels to catch any excess oil before serving.
9. Serve with your favorite dipping sauce.

Spicy Carrot Egg Rolls

Serves: 12
Preparation time: 1 hour 15 minutes
Cooking time: 10 minutes

Ingredients:

4 carrots, shredded

1 celery stalk, finely-chopped

3 cloves garlic, minced

2 tablespoons fresh ginger, grated

1 lime, juiced

2 green onions, chopped

¼ cup low-sodium soy sauce

4 tablespoons hot pepper sauce

1 cup fresh cilantro leaves, chopped

1 egg, beaten

Extra light olive oil

12 egg roll wrappers

Preparation:

1. Combine carrots, celery, ginger, garlic, lime juice, green onions, soy sauce, and hot pepper sauce in large bowl, and refrigerate for an hour.
2. Place egg roll wrapper on a flat surface with one corner pointed at you.

3. Place one tablespoon of carrot filling and a little cilantro about three inches above bottom corner, roll bottom corner over wrapper and fold over the left side and then the right side over the wrapper, continue to roll up to one inch below the top corner, brush the top edges with egg wash and seal wrapper, repeat.
4. Fill a heavy frying pot halfway with oil or you can also fry the eggrolls in a wok. Let the oil reach 350°F/177°C. Deep fry egg rolls until golden brown, about 2-3 minutes per side. You can also use a deep frying machine.
5. Place egg rolls on plate lined with paper towels to catch any excess oil before serving.
6. Serve with your favorite dipping sauce.

Mixed Egg Roll

Serves: 20
Preparation time: 45 minutes
Chilling time: 4 hours
Cooking time: 20 minutes

Ingredients:
¼ pound ground pork
¼ pound ground chicken or turkey
2 tablespoons olive oil
4 tablespoons vegetable oil,
1 cup green cabbage finely, chopped
1 carrot finely, shredded
1 onion finely, diced
1 cup bean sprout
2 teaspoons garlic minced
2 teaspoons fresh ginger, grated
2 teaspoons soya sauce
1 teaspoon chili sauce
Salt and pepper
20 egg roll wraps
Oil for frying

Preparation:

1. In a mixing bowl, mix the pork and chicken. Add salt to the mixture, and 2 tablespoons of olive oil. Let it marinate for 30 minutes.
2. Warm a pan on medium-high heat. Add 2 tablespoons of vegetable oil.
3. Once the oil has heated, add ginger and garlic to it. Fry for 30 seconds to a 1 minute.
4. Add the meat mixture to it, and fry till the color changes and the meat is cooked through.
5. Remove the meat mixture from the pan. Add two more tablespoons of vegetable oil to the pan.
6. Fry the vegetables. Season with salt and pepper to taste.
7. Mix in 2 teaspoons of soya sauce and 1 teaspoon of chili sauce.
8. Once the vegetables have cooked thoroughly, add the meat mixture back in. Stir until well combined.
9. Remove from heat, and let it cool down.
10. Keep the egg roll wraps on a flat surface.
11. Spread the mixture as per your liking on each one of them.
12. Wrap the rolls, and refrigerate them for 4 hours.
13. Cover them with a plastic wrap so that they do not dry. After 4 hours, fry them to get crispy and tasty egg rolls.

Mushrooms and Beef Egg Roll

Serving: 10
Preparation time: 20 minutes
Cooking time: 35 minutes

Ingredients:

1 onion, diced
1 tablespoon olive oil
2 baby Bella mushrooms, chopped
½ pound ground beef
4 teaspoons soya sauce
1 cup green cabbage, shredded
1 teaspoon chili garlic sauce
2 teaspoons ground black pepper, fresh
10 egg roll wrappers defrosted
1 teaspoon sesame oil
1 tablespoon water, 1 egg, beaten together
Oil for frying

Preparation:

1. In a frying pan or a wok, warm the olive oil on medium heat. Add the beef.
2. Cook the beef till it browns, around 8-10 minutes.
3. Add onions, mushrooms, and cabbage to pan. Stir-fry for another 5 minutes.

4. Remove the pan from the heat, and add soya sauce, chili garlic sauce, and sesame oil.
5. Mix it all thoroughly, and let it cool.
6. Take an egg roll wrap and place it on a dry and flat surface.
7. Place around 2-3 tablespoons of the mixture in the middle of the wrap.
8. Roll the wrap tightly and seal the ends using the egg and water mixture.
9. Do the same for all the wraps.
10. Place a large saucepan on medium heat, and put some oil into it so it covers the egg roll completely, about 2 inches. You can also use a frying machine.
11. Once the oil has heated to 350°F/177°C, fry the egg rolls in batches. Do not overcrowd the saucepan.
12. Fry on all sides till golden and crisp.

Turon Saba *(Filipino Dessert Egg Roll)*

Serves: 16
Preparation time: 15 minutes
Cooking time: 10 minutes

Ingredients:

4 plantains
1 jackfruit, peeled, chopped
½ cup cane sugar
16 egg roll wrappers
Extra light olive oil
1 tablespoon flour
2 tablespoons water
16 egg roll wrappers

Preparation:

1. Mix water, flour, set aside.
2. Slice plantain into ¼" thick slices and tolls with jackfruit.
3. Place ¼ cup of the mixture onto egg roll wrapper and sprinkle with brown sugar.
4. Fill a cast iron pot half way up with extra light olive oil and place over medium heat.
5. Place egg roll wrapper on a flat surface with one corner pointed at you.

6. Place one heaping tablespoon of filling about three inches above bottom corner, roll bottom corner over wrapper and fold over the left side and then the right side over the wrapper, continue to roll up to one inch below the top corner, brush the top edges with water and flour mixture and seal wrapper, repeat.
7. Oil should be at a temperature of 350°F/177°C before you begin frying the egg rolls. Once it is ready, place egg rolls in oil and sprinkle each one with a little cane sugar, cook for a minute, turn over and sprinkle with a little more cane sugar, cook until golden brown.
8. Serve with Caramel dipping sauce.

COLD SPRING ROLLS RECIPES

Vietnamese Fresh Spring Roll

Yields: 8 spring rolls
Preparation time: 50 minutes
Cooking time: none

Ingredients:

8 rice wrappers

8 large cooked shrimp, cut in half

3 tablespoons fresh mint leaves

8 lettuce leaves

½ cup Thai basil leaves

3 tablespoons fresh cilantro

4 teaspoons fish sauce

2 ounces rice vermicelli

1 tablespoon fresh lime juice

1 clove garlic, minced

½ teaspoon chili sauce

1 tablespoons hoisin sauce

2 tablespoons crushed peanuts

Water

Preparation:
1. Cook the rice vermicelli according to package instructions.
2. Drain the water. Place the vermicelli in a bowl. Add the fish sauce, lime juice, garlic, chili sauce, and hoisin sauce. Mix well. Set vermicelli aside.
3. Prepare all your ingredients at arm's reach of the working surface where you will prepare the rolls.
4. Fill a large enough bowl with warm water to fit the rice paper.
5. Dip the wraps one by one in the water for a few seconds.
6. Once soft, place on a dry and flat surface.
7. At the center of the wrapper, start layering the ingredients one by one. Start with the lettuce leaves, then the shrimp, basil leaves, mint, cilantro, crushed peanuts, and finish with the vermicelli.
8. Leave enough space for folding. For the fresh spring roll folding method, go to page 13. Roll the wrap from one end to the other to seal the ingredients inside.
9. Serve with peanut sauce.

Avocado and Mandarine Spring Rolls

Serves: 16
Preparation time: 20 minutes
Cooking time: none

Ingredients:

1 avocado, pitted, peeled
2 mandarin oranges, peeled, segmented
½ cup bean sprouts
1 green onion, chopped
½ cup green cabbage, chopped
1 cup cooked vermicelli noodles
1 tablespoon fresh ginger, grated
¼ cup pure orange juice
¼ cup low-sodium soy sauce
16 rice paper wrappers
4 tablespoons sesame oil

Preparation:

1. Fill a medium-sized bowl with warm water, set aside.
2. Slice avocado into 1/2" cubes and place in bowl with Mandarin orange segments, bean sprouts, green onions, cabbage, and Vermicelli noodles.

3. In a second bowl combine soy sauce, ginger, 4 tablespoons sesame oil, and orange juice. Mix well.
4. Stir in the orange dressing with avocado mixture, let sit for 10 minutes, and then drain any excess liquid.
5. Place one rice wrapper in bowl of warm water for 15 seconds or until pliable.
12. Place rice wrapper on flat surface, spoon 1 tablespoon of mixture on the rice paper on the side closest to you and 2" from the bottom of the paper. For the complete spring roll folding technique, turn to page 13.
6. Roll the paper over the filling and roll halfway up, then fold the left side and right side over the filling, continue rolling to top, use a little extra water if needed to seal the top.
7. Serve with a dipping sauce like the quick and easy orange dipping sauce.

Roasted Pork Spring Rolls

Serves: 15 to 20 rolls
Preparation time: 1 hour
Marinating time: 2-4 hours
Cooking time: 40 minutes

Ingredients:

2 pounds pork loin roast

1 red pepper, sliced

1 English cucumber, sliced lengthwise

1 bunch basil leaves

Lettuce leaves

Rice papers

Pork marinade ingredients

3 cloves garlic minced

1 minced shallot

1 Thai chilies, diced

1 tablespoon fish Sauce

2 tablespoon soya sauce

1 teaspoon brown sugar

¼ cup vegetable oil

2 teaspoons black pepper, grounded

Preparation:
1. Mix all the marinade ingredients in a sealable bag. Add the pork loins. Marinate for at least 2 to 4 hours in the refrigerator.
2. Preheat the oven to 350°F/177°C.
3. Place the pork on a roasting pan, and bake in the oven for 30-40 minutes until the pork is cooked through. Internal temperature should reach 145°F/63°C on a meat thermometer.
4. Remove from the oven and let rest for 30 minutes.
5. Slice the pork in thin slices.
6. Wet the rice paper in lukewarm water on by one.
7. Spread them properly on a flat surface.
8. Layer the ingredients on the wrapper, starting with the lettuce leave.
9. Roll the paper and seal the ingredients inside.

Peach Spring Rolls

Serves: 4 pieces
Preparation time: 15 minutes
Cooking time: none

Ingredients:

2 peaches, peeled and pitted

2 cups lettuce, shredded

1 small cucumber

Fresh basil

Fresh mint

Fresh cilantro

¼ cup raw cashews, chopped

4 rice paper sheets

Preparation:

1. Take a bowl full of lukewarm water.
2. Dip the rice papers in it the water to soften them.
3. Spread them on a flat surface to start filling them.
4. Starting from the center, layer the ingredients on the rice paper.
5. Start rolling the wrappers from one end.
6. Firmly fold in the sides.
7. You can slice each of them into halves before you serve.

Asparagus Spring Roll

Serves: 10 pieces
Preparation time: 30 minutes
Cooking time: 8 minutes

Ingredients:

1 bunch small asparagus

1 tablespoon olive oil

Black pepper

12 crisp bacon slices

1 cucumber, thinly sliced

1 carrot, thinly sliced

Lettuce

Fresh basil

Fresh mint

10 rice wrappers

Preparation:

1. Start by setting the oven at 400°F/204°C.
2. Arrange the asparagus in a single row on a baking sheet. Sprinkle about 1 tablespoon of olive oil over the asparagus. Season with salt and pepper. Roast in the oven for 5-8 minutes until the asparagus are just tender.
3. Remove from the oven and allow to cool down.

4. In the meantime, prepare all your ingredients, and fill a shallow dish with warm water to soften the rice wrappers.
5. Soften the rice wrappers one at a time, and place it on a clean working surface.
6. Layer all your ingredients on the wrapper starting with the lettuce leaves, then the asparagus, bacon strip, cucumber slices, carrot slices, basil and mint leaves.
7. Fold the rolls as shown before. Turn to page 13 for folding instructions.

Apple and Chicken Spring Rolls

Serves: 6
Preparation time: 20 minutes
Cooking time: none

Ingredients:
6 rice paper wraps
6 strips cooked chicken breast
12 strips apple
1 carrot, thinly chopped
6 lettuce leaves like butter lettuce
2 tablespoons cilantro leaves

Preparation:
1. Dip the rice wraps in warm water and soften them one by one.
2. Place them on a flat surface to start filling them.
3. Layer the ingredients on the wrapper, starting with the lettuce leaves, then the chicken, apples, carrot and cilantro.
4. Start rolling from the edge that is closest to the ingredients.
5. Seal the bases by rolling them up.
6. Sprinkle some sesame seeds on the top and serve.

Ginger Chicken Spring Rolls

Serves: 16
Preparation time: 35 minutes
Cooking time: none

Ingredients:

1 cup roasted chicken, shredded
1 small carrot, shredded
1 cup bamboo shoots
½ cup green cabbage, shredded
½ cup bean sprouts
¼ cup low-sodium soy sauce
16 rice paper wrappers
Sesame oil

Preparation:

1. Fill a medium-sized bowl with warm water, set aside.
2. Chop cashews and combine in bowl with soy sauce and ginger, set aside.
3. In a second bowl, combine chicken, carrot, bamboo shoots, green cabbage and bean sprouts.
4. Combine gingered cashews with chicken, and marinate for 20 minutes.

5. Place one rice wrapper in bowl of warm water for 15 seconds or until pliable.
6. Place rice wrapper on flat surface, spoon 1 tablespoon of mixture on the rice paper on the side closest to you and 2" from the bottom of the paper.
7. Roll the paper over the filling and roll halfway up, then fold the left side and right side over the filling, continue rolling to top. Use a little extra water if needed to seal the top.

Green Papaya Spring Rolls

Serves: 18
Preparation time: 30 minutes
Cooking time: none

Ingredients:

1 green papaya
1 cup bean sprouts
1 small carrot, shredded
1 cup coriander, chopped
¼ cup organic peanut butter
1 tablespoon fish sauce
4 tablespoons low-sodium soy sauce
1 lime, juiced
18 rice paper wrappers
Sesame oil

Preparation:

1. Fill a medium-sized bowl with warm water, set aside.
2. Peel papaya, remove pit, and slice into ½" cubes.
3. Combine papaya, bean sprouts, carrot, and coriander in one bowl.
4. In a second bowl, whisk together fish sauce, soy sauce, peanut butter, and lime juice

5. Place one rice wrapper in bowl of warm water for 15 seconds or until pliable.
6. Place rice wrapper on flat surface, spoon 1 tablespoon of mixture on the rice paper on the side closest to you and 2" from the bottom of the paper.
7. Roll the paper over the filling and roll halfway up, then fold the left side and right side over the filling, continue rolling to top. Use a little extra water if needed to seal the top.

Rice Paper Recipe

Ingredients:

Rice flour

Water

Equipment:

Stock pot with cover

Quilting hoop the size of the pot

Cheese cloth

Preparation:

1. Make a thick paste of the rice and water.
2. Pour the rice flour into water slowly, to make a glue-like paste.
3. Fill a stockpot with water and bring it to a boil on high heat.
4. Tighten the cheese cloth on the hoop and place it on the stock pot.
5. Pour some mixture on the cheese cloth and spread in a circular motion using the back of the spoon.
6. Cover the stock pot, and let the rice paper steam for about 1 minute.
7. With a long bamboo stick, roll out the rice paper from the cloth and place it on a cooling rack.

8. Repeat the same steps to make as many rice papers as you need.
9. Let it dry for half a day. Store in a dry place.

FRIED AND BAKED SPRING ROLLS RECIPES

Vietnamese Spring Roll

Serves: 20
Preparation time: 15 minutes
Cooking time: 30 minutes

Ingredients:

½ pound pork

½ pound shrimp

½ cup taro root, shredded

2 carrots, peeled, shredded

2 green onions, finely chopped

4 cloves garlic, minced

½ cup mung bean sprouts

1 tablespoon fish sauce

3 tablespoons soy sauce

1 tablespoon cane sugar

1 tablespoon coarse black pepper

20 spring roll wrappers

Egg wash for sealing

Oil for frying

Preparation:
1. Place shrimp in blender and mix into a paste, add pork mix.
2. Place taro root, carrots, green onion, and mung beans sprouts in a large bowl. Add shrimp and pork, mix.
3. Add remaining ingredients into bowl, combine well.
4. Open your package of spring rolls and place all but one wrapper under a clean, damp, dish cloth to ensure wrappers do not dry out.
5. Set your wrapper on flat surface with one corner pointed at you.
6. Place a tablespoon of filling on the bottom of the wrapper, about two inches above the corner point.
7. Fold the bottom part of the wrapper over the filling, then fold the sides over the filling, so you have what almost looks like an envelope with a long flap.
8. Roll the spring roll away from you until you get about two inches from the top, brush the edges at the top with your egg wash, complete roll. Repeat.
9. Once you have all of your rolls set, line a plate with paper towels.

10. Fill a heavy pot halfway up with oil for frying. Warm the oil on medium heat until it reaches 350°F/177°C. You can also use a wok or a deep frying machine. Deep fry spring rolls until golden, about 1-2 minutes on each side.
11. Place spring rolls on a plate lined with paper towels to catch any excess oil before serving.
12. Serve with your favorite dipping sauce like honey ginger.

Shrimp Spring Rolls

Serves: 16
Preparation time: 20 minutes
Cooking time: 15 minutes

Ingredients:

½ pound shrimp

1 cup dry rice noodles

1 medium carrot, shredded

1 cup bean sprouts

½ cup cabbage, shredded

2 cloves, garlic, minced

1 cup low-sodium soy sauce

¼ cup oyster sauce

1 egg

16 spring roll wrappers

4 tablespoons sesame oil

Oil for frying

Preparation:

1. Cook rice noodles according to individual package directions. Drain and set aside.
2. Heat 4 tablespoons sesame oil in skillet or a wok, add shrimp and cook until pink.
3. Remove shrimp from skillet, and reserve. Add vegetables, and sauté until tender (3-4 minutes).

4. Return shrimp to skillet, add oyster sauce, combine, and set aside.
5. Open your package of spring rolls and place all but one wrapper under a clean, damp, dish cloth to ensure wrappers do not dry out.
6. Set your wrapper on flat surface with one corner pointed at you.
7. Place a tablespoon of filling on the bottom of the wrapper, about two inches above the corner point.
8. Fold the bottom part of the wrapper over the filling, and then fold the sides over the filling, so you have what almost looks like an envelope with a long flap.
9. Roll the spring roll away from you until you get about two inches from the top, brush the edges at the top with your egg wash, complete roll and repeat.
10. Once you have all of your rolls set, line a plate with paper towels.
11. Fill a heavy pot halfway up with oil for frying. Warm the oil on medium heat until it reaches 350ºF /177ºC. You can also use a wok or a deep frying machine. Deep fry spring rolls until golden, about 1-2 minutes on each side.
12. Place spring rolls on a plate lined with paper towels to catch any excess oil before serving.
13. Serve with your favorite dipping sauce.

Vegetable Lumpia

Serves: 16
Preparation time: 15 minutes
Cooking time: 15 minutes

Ingredients:

1½ cups tofu, firm

1 carrot, grated

1 cup bean sprouts

1½ cups cabbage, grated

1 spring onion, chopped

2 cloves, garlic, minced

1 cup low-sodium soy sauce

¼ cup oyster sauce

1 egg

16 spring roll wrappers

4 tablespoons sesame oil

Vegetable oil for frying

Preparation:

1. Heat 4 tablespoons of sesame oil in a skillet or a wok, add onion and garlic, and sauté for 30 seconds.
2. Add remaining vegetables, and sauté until tender (3-4 minutes).

3. Add soaked noodles, soy sauce, and oyster sauce into skillet and combine, set aside.
4. Open your package of spring rolls, and place all but one wrapper under a clean, damp, dish cloth to ensure wrappers do not dry out.
5. Set your wrapper on flat surface with one corner pointed at you.
6. Place a tablespoon of filling on the bottom of the wrapper, about two inches above the corner point.
7. Fold the bottom part of the wrapper over the filling, and then fold the sides over the filling, so you have what almost looks like an envelope with a long flap.
8. Roll the spring roll away from you until you get about two inches from the top, brush the edges at the top with your egg wash, complete roll. Repeat.
9. Fill a heavy pot halfway up with oil for frying. Warm the oil on medium heat until it reaches 350ºF/177ºC. You can also use a wok or a deep frying machine. Deep fry spring rolls until golden, about 1-2 minutes on each side.
10. Place spring rolls on a plate lined with paper towels to catch any excess oil before serving.
11. Serve with your favorite dipping sauce.

Hoisin Chicken Spring Rolls

Serves: 16
Preparation time: 15 minutes
Cooking time: 15 minutes

Ingredients:

1 cup cooked chicken, shredded
1 carrot, grated
1 cup bean sprouts
1½ cups cabbage, grated
2 spring onions, chopped
1 tablespoon ginger, grated
1 cup low-sodium soy sauce
¼ cup hoisin sauce
1 egg
16 spring roll wrappers
4 tablespoons sesame oil
Vegetable oil for frying

Preparation:

1. Heat 4 tablespoons of sesame oil in a skillet or a wok. Add onion, ginger, and sauté for 30 seconds.
2. Add remaining vegetables, sauté until tender (3-4 minutes).

3. Add soy sauce and hoisin sauce into skillet and combine, set aside.
4. Open your package of spring rolls and place all but one wrapper under a clean, damp, dish cloth to ensure wrappers do not dry out.
5. Set your wrapper on flat surface with one corner pointed at you.
6. Place a tablespoon of filling on the bottom of the wrapper, about two inches above the corner point.
7. Fold the bottom part of the wrapper over the filling, and then fold the sides over the filling – so you have what almost looks like an envelope with a long flap.
8. Roll the spring roll away from you until you get about two inches from the top, brush the edges at the top with your egg wash, complete roll and repeat.
9. Fill a heavy pot halfway up with oil for frying. Warm the oil on medium heat until it reaches 350°F /177°C. You can also use a wok or a deep frying machine. Deep fry spring rolls until golden, about 1-2 minutes on each side.
10. Place spring rolls on a plate lined with paper towels to catch any excess oil before serving.
11. Serve with your favorite dipping sauce.

Sesame Vegetable Spring Rolls

Serves: 16
Preparation time: 15 minutes
Cooking time: 15 minutes

Ingredients:

1 red bell pepper, seeded, julienned

1 carrot, julienned

1 cup bean sprouts

1 cup cabbage, grated

¼ cup water chestnuts, chopped

2 cloves, garlic, minced

1 cup Chow Mein noodles

1 cup low-sodium soy sauce

1 tablespoon cane sugar

1 tablespoon tahini

1 egg

4 tablespoons sesame oil

16 spring roll wrappers

Vegetable oil for frying

Preparation:

1. Place Chow Mein noodles in warm water, set aside.
2. Whisk egg in a bowl, set aside.

3. Heat 4 tablespoons sesame oil in skillet, add onion, garlic, and sauté for 30 seconds.
4. Add remaining vegetables, sauté until tender (3-4 minutes).
5. Add chestnuts, soaked noodles, soy sauce, tahini, and cane sugar into skillet, combine, set aside.
6. Open your package of spring rolls and place all but one wrapper under a clean, damp, dish cloth to ensure wrappers do not dry out.
7. Set your wrapper on flat surface with one corner pointed at you.
8. Place a tablespoon of filling on the bottom of the wrapper, about two inches above the corner point.
9. Fold the bottom part of the wrapper over the filling, and then fold the sides over the filling, so you have what almost looks like an envelope with a long flap.
10. Roll the spring roll away from you until you get about two inches from the top, brush the edges at the top with your egg wash, complete roll and repeat. Place the spring rolls in a plate and cover with a damp kitchen towel to avoid drying.
11. Fill a heavy pot halfway up with oil for frying. Warm the oil on medium heat until it reaches 350ºF/177ºF. You can also use a wok or a deep frying machine. Deep fry spring rolls until golden, about 1-2 minutes on each side.

12. Place spring rolls on a plate lined with paper towels to catch any excess oil before serving.
13. Serve with your favorite dipping sauce.

Baked Pork Spring Rolls

Serves: 18
Preparation time: 15 minutes
Cooking time: 15 minutes

Ingredients:

1 pound ground pork
1 red bell pepper, seeded, julienned
1 large carrot, peeled, shredded
½ cup green cabbage shredded
¼ cup Thai basil, chopped
1 cup Vermicelli noodles, cooked and chopped
½ cup cilantro, chopped
1 lime, juiced
1 tablespoon ginger, grated
2 tablespoons low-sodium soy sauce
1 clove garlic, minced
1 egg
18 Spring Roll wrappers
4 tablespoons extra virgin olive oil
Egg wash for sealing

Preparation:

1. Whisk egg, set aside.

2. Warm 4 tablespoons of extra virgin olive oil in skillet or wok over medium heat. Add onion and garlic, and sauté for 30 seconds to 1 minute.
3. Add ground pork, and brown. Remove from heat and place pork in a bowl. Reserve.
4. Add into skillet, red bell pepper, carrot, green cabbage, Thai basil, and cilantro. Sauté until the vegetables are tender, about 3-4 minutes.
5. Place vegetable mix into the bowl with the pork.
6. In a small bowl, combine lime juice, ginger, and soy sauce, and toss sauce with pork mixture.
7. Preheat oven to 425°F/218°C and place a sheet of parchment paper on baking tray.
8. Open your package of spring rolls and place all but one wrapper under a clean, damp, dish cloth to ensure wrappers do not dry out.
9. Set your wrapper on flat surface with one corner pointed at you.
10. Place a tablespoon of filling and ¼ tablespoon of vermicelli noodles on the bottom of the wrapper, about two inches above the corner point.
11. Fold the bottom part of the wrapper over the filling, and then fold the sides over the filling, so you have what almost looks like an envelope with a long flap. Go to page 13 for the spring roll folding method.

12. Roll the spring roll away from you until you get about two inches from the top, brush the edges at the top with your egg wash, complete roll and place on baking sheet. Repeat.
13. Place baking tray into the oven for 20 minutes, turn halfway through. The spring roll should be golden brown.
14. Remove from oven and serve hot with your favorite dipping sauce.

DUMPLING RECIPES

Asian food without dumplings is like eating Italian cuisine without pasta!

Dumpling Dough Recipes

The dumpling dough is the soul of this Asian specialty. Learn how to make it correctly, and your dumplings will be simply awesome. The dough required for steamed dumplings is different than the one used for fried dumplings. For the steamed ones, the dough has to be thicker and made with cold water, whereas the fried dumplings need thinner dough made with hot water Also, the dough can be kneaded by hand or in a food processor.

Serves: 32 Medium dumplings

Ingredients:
2 cups all-purpose flour
½ teaspoon salt (optional)
¾ cup boiled water or cold water depending of the kind of dumpling you want to make. The fried dumpling is steamed then fried

Preparation:

1. Add flour and salt, if using, to a large mixing bowl.
2. Slowly add water to it.
3. After adding all of the water, start kneading the dough slowly.
4. If the dough isn't easy to knead, add some more water with a spoon.
5. Now transfer the dough onto a flat lightly-floured surface.
6. Knead it further to make a smooth and elastic dough.
7. Cover the dough in plastic wrap, and let it rest for 30 minutes before using.
8. You can refrigerate it and use later for up to 3-4 days.

Pork and Shrimp Dumpling

Serves: 20 pieces
Preparation time: 20 minutes
Cooking time: 1 hour

Ingredients:

½ pound ground pork
8-10 medium shrimps, cooked and chopped finely
1 scallion stalk, finely chopped
1 teaspoon Shaoxing wine
½ teaspoon salt
½ teaspoon soya sauce
½ teaspoon sesame oil
1 1-inch ginger, grated
20 dumpling wrappers

Preparation:

1. Start with mixing all the dry ingredients and seasonings
2. With the mixture ready, you can now begin to fill in the dumplings.
3. Take a dumpling wrapper and place the mixture at the center.
4. Now wet the edges of the wrapper and fold the dumpling, making proper pleats.

5. Place them in a steamer and cook for 8-10 minutes. Turn to page 26 for the bamboo steamer cooking method
6. Serve with a dipping sauce like the classic soy and vinegar dipping sauce.

Pepper Pork Dumplings

Serves: 14
Preparation time: 15 minutes
Cooking time: 15 minutes

Ingredients:

¾ pound ground pork

¾ cup green cabbage

1 green onion, minced

1 tablespoon ginger, grated

4 tablespoons low-sodium soy sauce

1 teaspoon black pepper

1 egg, beaten

Extra light olive oil

14 Dumpling wrappers

Preparation:

1. Heat light olive oil in skillet over medium heat.
2. Add ground pork and brown.
3. Add ginger, onion, sauté for a minute.
4. Add soy sauce, black pepper, and green cabbage, mix, and remove from heat.
5. Place a tablespoon of filling in the center of the dumpling wrapper, then brush the top half circle edge with beaten egg.

6. Bring the bottom half up over the filling to meet the top half, and pinch the two halves together all along the sides, and give a second pinch over to ensure there are no air holes.
7. Place dumplings on a plate and cover with a slightly damp cloth to ensure they do not dry out.
8. Fill a large pot of water up halfway over medium heat and bring to a boil.
9. Leave raw dumplings under damp cloth.
10. Place the dumpling in a prepared steamer and cook for 15 minutes. Turn to page 26 for the bamboo steamer cooking method.
11. Serve warm with your favorite dipping sauce.

Beef and Caramelized Scallion Fried Dumplings

Serves: 14
Preparation time: 15 minutes
Cooking time: 15 minutes

Ingredients:

¾ pound ground beef

1 cup mung beans sprouts, roughly chopped

3 scallions, finely-chopped

1 tablespoon ginger, grated

4 tablespoons low-sodium soy sauce

1 teaspoon black pepper

1 egg, beaten

Extra light olive oil

14 dumpling wrappers

Preparation:

1. Heat light olive oil in skillet over medium heat, add scallions, sauté for 30 seconds.
2. Sprinkle scallions with brown sugar, give a quick sauté.
3. Add ground beef and brown.
4. Add ginger, scallions, sauté for a minute.

5. Add soy sauce, black pepper, mung bean sprouts, and green cabbage, mix and remove from heat.
6. Place a tablespoon of filling in the center of the dumpling wrapper. Brush the top half circle edge with egg wash.
7. Bring the bottom half up over the filling to meet the top half and pinch the two halves together in the center, then pinch together the sides.
8. Place dumplings on a plate and cover with a slightly damp cloth to ensure they do not dry out.
9. Fill a large pot of water up halfway over medium heat and bring to a boil.
10. Drop a batch of dumplings into the water and cook for 10 minutes. Leave raw dumplings under damp cloth,
11. Warm 1-2 tablespoons of olive oil in a large skillet. Once the dumplings are cooked, fry them in small batches in the heated skillet until golden brown.
12. Serve warm with a dipping sauce like the spicy peanut sauce.

Spicy Shrimp Dumplings

Serves: 14
Preparation time: 15 minutes
Cooking time: 15 minutes

Ingredients:

¾ pound shrimp, shelled, deveined
1 red chili pepper, seeded, chopped
1 red bell pepper, seeded, julienned
1 green onion, minced
1 tablespoon ginger, grated
4 tablespoons low-sodium soy sauce
2 tablespoons Sriracha
1 teaspoon black pepper
1 egg
Extra light olive oil
14 dumpling wrappers

Preparation:

1. Heat light olive oil in skillet over medium heat.
2. Add ginger, onion, sauté for a minute.
3. Add shrimp and sauté until pink.
4. Mix soy sauce, Sriracha, black pepper and green cabbage with skillet mixture, remove from heat.

5. Place a tablespoon of filling in the center of the dumpling wrapper, then brush the edges with egg wash.
6. Bring the bottom half up over the filling to meet the top half, and pinch the two halves together all along the sides, give a second pinch over to ensure there are no air holes.
7. Place dumplings on a plate and cover with a slightly damp cloth to ensure they do not dry out.
8. Fill a large pot of water up halfway over medium heat, and bring to a boil.
9. Drop a batch of dumplings into the water and cook for 10 minutes. Leave raw dumplings under damp cloth. You can also steam them for 15 minutes in a bamboo steamer.

Thai Trifecta Dumplings

Serves: 14
Preparation time: 15 minutes
Cooking time: 20 minutes

Ingredients:

½ pound shrimp, peeled, deveined

½ pound pork

¼ pound crab

¾ cup green cabbage, shredded

1 green onion, minced

5 cloves garlic, grated

4 tablespoons low-sodium soy sauce

1 teaspoon black pepper

Extra light olive oil

14 dumpling wrappers

Preparation:

1. Place shrimp and crab into blender and mix into paste.
2. Add pork into shrimp mixture and mix.
3. Heat light olive oil in skillet over medium heat.
4. Add garlic, onion, sauté for 30 seconds. Add shrimp/crab/pork mixture and continue to sauté until browned.

5. Add soy sauce, black pepper, and green cabbage. Mix and remove from heat.
6. Place a tablespoon of filling in the center of the dumpling wrapper, then brush the top half circle edge with your flour mixture.
7. Bring the bottom half up over the filling to meet the top half and pinch the two halves together all along the sides, give a second pinch over to ensure there are no air holes.
8. Place dumplings on a plate and cover with a slightly damp cloth to ensure they do not dry out.
9. Fill a large pot of water up halfway over medium heat and bring to a boil.
10. Drop a batch of dumplings into the water and cook for 8 minutes. Leave raw dumplings under damp cloth. You can also steam the dumplings in a bamboo steamer for 10-15 minutes.

Mushroom Dumplings

Serves: 14
Preparation time: 10 minutes
Cooking time: 15 minutes

Ingredients:

10 button mushrooms, chopped

¼ cup bamboo shoots

1 cup green cabbage

1 green onion, minced

1 tablespoon ginger, grated

4 tablespoons low-sodium soy sauce

1 teaspoon black pepper

Extra light olive oil

14 dumpling wrappers

Preparation:

1. Heat light olive oil in skillet over medium heat.
2. Add mushroom, onion, garlic, and sauté for a minute.
3. Add soy sauce, black pepper, bamboo shoots, and green cabbage, mix and remove from heat.
4. Place a tablespoon of filling in the center of the dumpling wrapper, then brush the top half circle edge with your flour mixture.

5. Bring the bottom half up over the filling to meet the top half and pinch the two halves together all along the sides, give a second pinch over to ensure there are no air holes.
6. Place dumplings on a plate and cover with a slightly damp cloth to ensure they do not dry out.
7. Fill a large pot of water up halfway over medium heat and bring to a boil.
11. Drop a batch of dumplings into the water and cook for 10 minutes. Leave raw dumplings under damp cloth. You can also steam the dumplings in a bamboo steamer for 15 minutes.

Curried Beef Dumplings

Serves: 18
Preparation time: 15 minutes
Cooking time: 20 minutes

Ingredients:

1 pound ground beef
1 red bell pepper, seeded, diced
1 green onion, minced
2 cloves garlic, minced
1 tablespoon ginger, grated
1 egg, beaten
¼ cup low-sodium soy sauce
1 teaspoon black pepper
1 teaspoon curry powder
Extra light olive oil
18 dumpling wrappers

Preparation:

1. Heat light olive oil in skillet over medium heat.
2. Add beef, garlic, onion, and sauté until beef is browned.
3. Add red bell pepper, ginger, soy sauce, black pepper, mix and remove from heat.

4. Place a tablespoon of filling in the center of the dumpling wrapper, now brush the top half circle edge with beaten egg.
5. Bring the bottom half up over the filling to meet the top half and pinch the two halves together all along the sides, give a second pinch over to ensure there are no air holes.
6. Place dumplings on a plate and cover with a slightly damp cloth to ensure they do not dry out.
7. Fill a large pot of water up halfway over medium heat and bring to a boil.
12. Drop a batch of dumplings into the water and cook for 10 minutes. Leave raw dumplings under damp cloth. You can also steam the dumplings in a bamboo steamer for 12-15 minutes.

Chicken and Leek Fried Dumplings

Serves: 16

Preparation time: 15 minutes

Cooking time: 10 minutes

Ingredients:

1 leek, chopped

2 cups roast chicken, chopped

1 cup shredded cabbage

1 tablespoon ginger root, grated

¼ cup rice wine

1 teaspoon salt

2 tablespoons soy sauce

1 egg, beaten with 1 tablespoon of water

Extra light olive oil

16 dumpling wrappers

Preparation:

1. Heat 3 tablespoons oil in skillet, add leek, sauté for a minute, and remove from heat.
2. Add roast chicken, cabbage, ginger root, rice wine, soy sauce, salt, and mix well.
3. Place a tablespoon of filling in the center of the dumpling wrapper, now brush the top half circle edge with beaten egg.

4. Bring the bottom half up over the filling to meet the top half and pinch the two halves together all along the sides, give a second pinch over to ensure there are no air holes.
5. Place dumplings on a plate and cover with a slightly damp cloth to ensure they do not dry out.
6. Fill a large pot of water up halfway over medium heat and bring to a boil.
7. Drop a batch of dumplings into the water and cook for 10 minutes. Leave raw dumplings under damp cloth. You can also steam the dumplings for 12-15 minutes.
8. Warm 1-2 tablespoons of olive oil in a large skillet. Once the dumplings are cooked, fry them in small batches in the heated skillet until golden brown.
9. Serve warm with a dumpling dipping sauce.

Classic Chinese Dumplings

Serves: 60 pieces
Preparation time: 1 hour 30 minutes
Cooking time: 30 minutes

Ingredients:

For Dumpling

3 cups all-purpose flour

1¼ cup cold water

¼ teaspoon salt

For Filling

1 pound ground pork

2 tablespoons soya sauce

1 teaspoon salt

1 tablespoon rice wine vinegar

¼ teaspoon white pepper

2 tablespoons sesame oil

2 tablespoons vegetable oil

3 green onions, sliced

1½ cup Napa cabbage, shredded

4 tablespoons bamboo shoots, shredded

1 teaspoon fresh ginger, grated

2 garlic cloves, minced

Egg wash for sealing

Preparation:
1. Start by making the dough. Mix the salt and the dough thoroughly on a large bowl. Slowly add the water and mix to form a ball of dough.
2. Knead the dough till it is extremely smooth and elastic. Cover it with a plastic wrap, and let it rest for 30 minutes.
3. While the dough is resting, prepare the filling. Add the pork to a large mixing bowl. Add the rice wine vinegar, salt, soy sauce, and white pepper. Mix thoroughly to ensure the consistency of the mixture. Set aside.
4. Warm 2 tablespoons of vegetable oil in a wok on medium-high heat. Add the garlic and ginger. Sauté for 30 seconds. Reduce heat to medium and add the green onions, Napa cabbage, and bamboo shoots. Sauté until the vegetables are tender. Remove from heat and let cool down for a few minutes.
5. Add the vegetable mixture to the pork. Mix well.
6. After half an hour, with a roll pin on a lightly floured working surface, roll the dough. Use a cookie cutter or a glass to make nice round even wrappers of about 2-2½-inch wide.
7. Place 1 teaspoon to 1½ teaspoon of the pork filling onto one half of the wrapper. Seal the dumpling by brushing lightly with some egg wash

on the edges. Press lightly to seal. Turn to page 21 for the complete dumpling folding method with pictures.

8. You can cook the dumplings by either steaming or boiling them.
9. When boiling, add them to the pot only when the water has started boiling. Let them boil for 12 minutes.
10. If you are using a bamboo steamer, place cabbage, bok choy or large lettuce leaves at the bottom of the steamer. It will prevent the dumplings from sticking to the bottom. Arrange the dumpling so they do not touch. Steam for 15 minutes. Turn to page 26 for the technique of using a bamboo steamer.
11. You can also fry them, after they have been boiled or steamed for added flavor.

Chicken Dumplings with Ginger-Coriander Dipping Sauce

Serves: 30
Preparation time: 20 minutes
Cooking time: 30 minutes

Ingredients:

Filling ingredients
1 cup ground chicken
1 onion, finely chopped
2 garlic cloves, minced
¼ cup bamboo shoots
2 teaspoons rice wine vinegar
¼ teaspoon white pepper
¾ teaspoon sesame oil
2 tablespoons grape seed oil
Salt
30 dumpling wrappers

Dipping sauce ingredients
½ inch piece fresh ginger, grated
½ cup reduced sodium soy sauce
1 tablespoon rice wine vinegar
1 pinch red chili flakes
3 teaspoons sugar
1 tablespoon fresh coriander leaves, chopped

Preparation:

1. Heat 2 tablespoons of grape seed oil in a wok on medium-high heat. Add onion and stir-fry for 1 minute. Add garlic and sauté for 1 minute, until fragrant and tender. Remove from heat.
2. In a large bowl, mix the minced chicken, rice wine vinegar, white pepper, oil, and bamboo shoot. Add cooked onions and garlic. Mix well.
3. Add salt to taste and mix thoroughly.
4. Take the dumpling wrappers and place them flat on your working surface.
5. Add 1 teaspoon of the chicken mixture to the center of the wrap. Fold to make pleats and seal the ends.
6. Steam these dumplings in a wok, double boiler, or a bamboo steamer for 15 minutes.
7. To make the dipping sauce, mix ginger, sugar vinegar, soya sauce, red chili flakes, and coriander in a container. Stir well.

Shanghai Dumplings

Serves: 32
Preparation time: 40 minutes
Cooking time: 20 minutes

Ingredients:

Dough ingredients

3 cups plus 2 tablespoons all-purpose flour

¾ cup boiling water

¼ cup cold water

1 tablespoon sunflower oil

Filling ingredients

1 pound ground pork

½ pound shelled and deveined shrimp, finely chopped

3 green onions, finely chopped

2 teaspoons white sugar

2 tablespoons soy sauce

2 teaspoons fresh ginger, grated

Salt and pepper

Preparation:

1. Add the flour to a food processor. Remove ¼ cup of it and it put it aside.
2. Add the boiling water slowly, and pulse until a stiff dough forms.

3. Add the cold water and the sunflower oil to it. Pulse until the dough becomes smooth and elastic. If it too wet and sticky, add some of the reserved flour. Pulse the dough a few more times until the dough is smooth. You can also make the dough manually. Just make sure to knead enough until you have a smooth and elastic dough.
4. Wrap the dough in a plastic wrap and let it rest for 30 minutes at room temperature.
5. In the meantime, make the filling. Add all the ingredients, one by one, in a large bowl. Season with salt and pepper. Mix thoroughly.
6. After half an hour has passed, divide the dough into 32 small, even pieces.
7. On a floured working surface, roll them using a rolling pin into very thin circular wrappers. Use a 4-inch round cookie cutter or a glass to make clean-cut wrappers.
8. Place the wrappers on a clean lightly floured working surface.
9. Add 1 generous tablespoon of the filling in the center of the wrapper. Brush lightly the edges of the wrapper around the filling with some water. Bring all the edges over the filling and seal by pinching the dough together.

10. Prepare a bamboo steamer and steam the dumplings for 15 minutes.
11. Serve the dumplings hot with a dumpling dipping sauce.

Mandu Dumplings (Korean dumplings)

Serves: about 50 large dumplings
Preparation time: 60 minutes
Cooking time: 60 minutes

Ingredients

Dough ingredients

5 cups all-purpose flour

1 teaspoon potato starch

½ teaspoon salt

1 tablespoon vegetable oil

1 cup warm water

1 egg

Filling ingredients

1 pound ground pork

1 pound ground beef

½ cup Asian garlic chives, chopped

4-5 shitake mushrooms, chopped

2 green onions, sliced

½ semi-firm tofu package, crumbled

2 cups kimchi

1 cup bean sprouts

2 oz. glass noodles

1 egg

3 cloves garlic, minced

1 tablespoon fresh ginger, minced

1 tablespoon sesame oil

1 tablespoon salt

½ teaspoon black pepper

1 egg white for sealing

Preparation:

1. Prepare the dough first. In a mixing bowl, add the flour, potato starch, and salt. Mix well. Add the egg and stir. Slowly add the water and knead the dough until you get an elastic, smooth dough. Cover with plastic wrap and let it rest at room temperature for 30 minutes.
2. With a rolling pin, roll the dough until it is very thin. Cut out the form of your dumpling with a round cookie cutter of about 4-inch wide.
3. While the dough is resting, you can prepare the filling. Prepare the glass noodles by immersing the dry noodle into a bowl of hot water. Let it rest for a few minutes until the noodles are soft. Drain to remove all the moisture you can from the noodles. Give the noodles a rough chop, and set aside.
4. Place the kimchi in a strainer and rinse under cold water. With cotton cheese cloth, remove all the moisture you can from the kimchi. Chop the kimchi finely.

5. With cotton cheese cloth remove all the moisture you can from the tofu. Chop and set aside.
6. Rinse the bean sprouts under cold water and drain and pat dry. Roughly chop.
7. Wash and trim the green onions and Asian garlic chives. Pat dry with paper towel to remove moisture. Slice both thinly and reserve.
8. In a large mixing bowl, add the pork, beef, salt, pepper, garlic, ginger, sesame oil, chopped kimchi, mushrooms, green onions, Asian garlic chives, bean sprouts, glass noodles, egg, and tofu. Mix it thoroughly.
9. Place the mandu wrappers on lightly floured working surface. Place about 1 tablespoon of the filling in the middle of each wrapper. Fold as desired and seal by brushing some of the egg white around the edges of the wrapper. Turn to page 21 for the complete dumpling folding technique.
10. Steam the dumplings in batches in a bamboo steamer or double boiler for 15-17 minutes.
11. If you like them crispy, fry in small batches in a large frying pan on medium heat until golden on all sides.
12. Serve with a spicy soy and vinegar dipping sauce.

Dim Sum Favorites

Dim sum is a style of eating in the Cantonese culture in which small, bite-sized portions of various dishes are served. The food that is generally served includes dumplings, rice buns, and noodle rolls that are filled with a variety of fillings. These are traditionally served in steam baskets. The best part of this arrangement is that this dish enables a person to taste a lot of options in a single serving. The following recipes are a few dim sum favorites.

"Chinesische Küche" by Kolumbusjogger
http://commons.wikimedia.org/wiki/File:Chinesische_K%C3%BCche.jpg#mediaviewer/File:Chinesische_K%C3%BCche.jpg

Baked Pineapple Buns

This is one of the most common desserts served at dim sum restaurants and parties other than egg tarts. Even though it's called pineapple buns, pineapple is not an ingredient in this recipe!

Serves: 15 buns
Preparation time: 80 minutes
Cooking time: 40 minutes

Ingredients:
<u>Bun ingredients</u>
4 cups flour
1 tablespoon quick rise dry yeast

2 tablespoons milk powder

⅓ cup superfine sugar

½ tablespoon salt

¼ cup unsalted butter

1¼ cups water

1 egg

Topping ingredients

⅓ cup butter

2 tablespoons shortening

½ cup powdered sugar

1 teaspoon pure vanilla extract

1 egg, beaten

1 cup all-purpose flour

Egg wash

1 egg

1 tablespoon water

Preparation:

1. To make the bun's dough, mix all the dry ingredients together in a large mixing bowl.
2. To this dry mixture, add the egg and water.
3. Continuously knead the dough and add butter to it.
4. Keep kneading till the dough turns smooth, elastic, and shiny.

5. Let the dough rest in a warm area, about 45-60 minutes. Cover with a damp kitchen towel. It should double in size.
6. In the meantime, prepare the topping. Beat the butter with powdered sugar, and vanilla essence with an electric mixer.
7. Add the egg followed by the flour.
8. Refrigerate the filling for about 15-20 minutes.

Making the Bun
1. Preheat the oven to 350°F /177°C.
2. Cut the bun dough into even pieces the size of a golf ball.
3. Form flat discs with each piece about ¾ inch thick.
4. Glaze the surface with the egg wash.
5. Place the topping on the dough disc and seal them, forming a ball.
6. With a sharp knife, score the top of the bun in a diamond-shaped pattern.
7. Brush with egg wash again.
8. Arrange the buns on a baking sheet with about 2-3 inches between each bun.
9. Place the baking sheet in the preheated oven, and bake for 35-40 minutes.

Steamed Barbeque Pork Buns

Serves: 16 buns
Preparation time: 60 minutes
Cooking time: 60 minutes

Ingredients:

Filling ingredients
- ½ cup chicken broth
- 2 tablespoons oyster sauce
- 2 tablespoons ketchup
- 5 tablespoons sugar
- 4 tablespoons cornstarch
- 1 tablespoon soy sauce
- 1 pork loin roast
- 2 tablespoons vegetable oil
- 1 yellow onion, chopped
- 1 tablespoon rice wine
- 1 tablespoon sesame oil
- Salt and pepper

Dough ingredients
- 2¼ cups all-purpose flour
- ½ cup white sugar
- 3½ teaspoons baking powder
- 6 tablespoons whole milk
- 2 tablespoons vegetable oil

Preparation:

Making the Filling

1. In a bowl, mix the broth, ketchup, oyster sauce, soy sauce, sugar, cornstarch, salt, and pepper. Mix them thoroughly and set aside.
2. Dice the pork into ¼-inch pieces to fill up around 1½ cups.
3. Heat a wok and add vegetable oil to it on medium-high heat. Once the oil is heated, add onions to the wok. Cook the onion till tender and golden brown, about 2-3 minutes.
4. Add the pork and cook for another 2-3 minutes. Add the rice wine vinegar to it and stir.
5. Reduce the heat to medium-low. Add the sauce. Keep stirring till the sauce thickens, 5-7 minutes. Remove from heat, and let the mixture cool.

Making the Dough

1. Mix the flour, sugar, and baking powder in a large bowl.
2. Slowly add milk to this mixture. Mix with your fingers. Add 3 tablespoons of water and continue kneading the dough.
3. Add some of the vegetable oil and continue kneading.
4. Knead the dough for another 10 minutes to make it very smooth.

5. If the dough is too sticky, sprinkle some flour on it and knead some more.
6. Let the dough rest for 60 minutes before you start making the buns.

Making the Buns
1. Divide the dough into 16 equal pieces. Make them into balls.
2. With your fingers, form a well in each dough ball so you can insert the filling.
3. Add the pork filling.
4. Pull the dough over the fillings to cover it completely and then twist the top to seal it completely.
5. Repeat the same for all the 16 buns.

Cooking the Buns
1. In a wok, boil approximately 6 cups of water.
2. Place some Napa cabbage leaves on the bottom of the bamboo steamer. Place your buns in. Remember not to crowd the steamers.
3. Place the steamers on the top of the wok to steam the buns.
4. Steam them continuously till they become fluffy and their top opens. This takes around 15-20 minutes.
5. Serve warm.

Fried Taro Dumplings

Servings: 24

Preparation time: 40 minutes

Cooking time: 20 minutes hour

Ingredients:

Dough ingredients

1¼ pound taro

¼ cup semi-salted butter, at room temperature

¼ pound wheat starch (also known as Tang flour, available in Asian food markets)

1 teaspoon baking soda

½ teaspoon salt

Filling ingredient

⅓ pound pork loin

⅓ pound shrimps, shelled and deveined

½ teaspoon Chinese five-spice seasoning

1 teaspoon soy sauce

1 teaspoon cornstarch

½ teaspoon sesame oil

5 fresh shitake mushrooms, washed and diced

1 green onion, finely sliced

2 garlic cloves, minced

¾ teaspoon chicken seasoning

¼ teaspoon white sugar

1 teaspoon wine vinegar

2 tablespoons grape seed oil

½ tablespoon cornstarch mixed with 1 tablespoon water

Oil for frying

Preparation:

1. To prepare the dough, peel the taro and slice. Steam the taro until tender, about 20-30 minutes. Place the taro in a large bowl, and mash it. Add baking soda, sugar, salt, wheat starch, and butter. Mix well and make sure there are no lumps in the dough.
2. Knead the dough until smooth and elastic. Separate the dough into 25 even pieces.

3. While the taro is cooking, dice the pork, shrimp, and mushrooms finely. Place in a large bowl, and add remaining ingredients. Let it rest for 15-20 minutes.
4. Heat 2 tablespoons of grape seed oil in the wok over medium-high heat. Sauté the filling mixture until the pork is cooked through and shrimp are pink. Add the cornstarch mix with water paste. Stir well. Remove from heat and let it cool down.
5. Fill each dough piece with some of the filling. Seal the top using your fingers and give the roll an oval shape similar to an egg.
6. Fill a heavy pot halfway up with oil for frying. Warm the oil on medium heat until it reaches 350°F/177°C. You can also use a wok or a deep frying machine. Fry these dumplings till the netting starts to appear on the surface of the dumplings, about 10-12 minutes.
7. Serve them hot.

Seafood Dim Sum Dumplings

Serves: 6
Preparation time: 45 minutes
Cooking time: 30 minutes

Ingredients:

Dim Sum filling

    2.5 oz Squid, cleaned

    10 oz king shrimp, shelled and deveined

    1 medium-sized carrot

    1 oz shitake mushrooms

    2 tablespoons corn flour

    2 tablespoons water

    3 tablespoons sesame oil

    ½ tablespoon superfine sugar

    Salt and black pepper

    1 package of dim sum wrapper

Dipping Sauce ingredients

    3 tablespoons light soya sauce

    3 tablespoons dark soya sauce

    1 teaspoon hot chili oil

    ½ teaspoon superfine sugar

    1 garlic clove, minced

Preparation:

1. Chop squid, shrimp, and mushrooms finely. Shred carrot.
2. Add carrot, corn flour, water, mushroom, sesame oil, shrimp, squid, and sugar in a bowl. Season with salt and pepper.
3. Mix all these ingredients, so that the consistency is thorough.
4. Pick a dim sum wrapper and spread it on your palms. Place some mixture at its center.
5. Wet the edges of the wrapper and accumulate it all at the top. Seal it by pinching it to make a pirate hat shape.
6. Repeat the same for all the wrappers.
7. Brush the wrapper with some oil and place it on a steamer.
8. Cook the dim sum for 5 minutes.
9. Make the dipping sauce by mixing all the sauce ingredients.
10. Garnish with baby herbs and mustard cress.

Dipping Sauces

Quick & Easy Peanut Sauce

Yields about ¾ cup

Ingredients:

5 tablespoons peanut butter

3 tablespoons water, warm

2 ½ tablespoons rice vinegar

1 ½ tablespoons soy sauce

3 teaspoons granulated sugar

Preparation:

1. Mix all the ingredients.
2. Store in an airtight container and refrigerate.
3. Refrigerate for at least 2 hours before using.
4. Add some warm water to the sauce before serving.
5. Use within 3-4 days.

Spicy Peanut Sauce

Yields about 1 ½ cup

Ingredients:

½ cup smooth organic peanut butter,

1 cup water

1 tablespoon soy sauce

1 tablespoon hoisin sauce

1 teaspoon chili paste

1 pinch hot chili pepper flakes

Preparation:
1. Combine ingredients in blender, mix until smooth
2. Add some more water if necessary for the desired consistency.

Note: this sauce can be very spicy depending on your chili paste. If you don't like spicy sauce, you can reduce the amount of chili paste and omit the chili pepper flakes. It is a good idea to taste the sauce and adjust the spiciness level to your own taste. You can start by adding only half of the chili paste and omit the chili pepper flakes. Then adjust to own liking.

Spicy Soy Dumpling Dipping Sauce

Yields about ¾ cup

Ingredients:

3 tablespoons light soya sauce

3 tablespoons dark soya sauce

3 tablespoons rice vinegar

1 teaspoon chili oil

½ teaspoon granulated sugar

1 garlic clove, minced

1 teaspoon ginger, grated

Preparation:

1. Mix all the ingredients in a container.
2. Store it in an airtight container.
3. Refrigerate it for 1 hour before serving.

Ginger Sauce

Yields about 1 cup

Ingredients:
½ cup soya sauce

¼ cup red wine

2 tablespoons brown sugar

2 green onions, chopped

Preparation:
1. In a bowl, add soya sauce, red wine and ginger, mix them thoroughly. Set aside.
2. Place a sauce pan on the flame and melt the brown sugar in it.
3. Add the soya sauce mixture to it.
4. Keep stirring constantly so that the mixture doesn't burn.
5. Boil the mixture and make sure that the brown sugar has melted completely.
6. Remove from heat and let it cool.
7. Add green onions to garnish and serve.

Hoisin Dipping Sauce

Yields about ¾ cup

Ingredients:
1 tablespoon olive oil

1 garlic clove, chopped

1 teaspoon ginger, chopped

6 tablespoons hoisin sauce

1 tablespoon dark soya sauce

2 tablespoons water

¼ teaspoons salt

½ teaspoon sesame oil

1½ tablespoon chili paste

1 tablespoon peanuts, chopped

Preparation:
1. Heat some oil in a wok on medium heat.
2. Add ginger and garlic to it.
3. Fry them till their color changes to golden brown, less than 1 minute.
4. Turn the flame to low and add all the other ingredients one by one.
5. Keep stirring constantly.
6. Bring to boil and remove from the flame.
7. Refrigerate it in an airtight container for 1 hour before serving.

Honey Mustard Dipping Sauce

Yields about ⅔ cup

Ingredients:

½ cup spicy brown mustard sauce

2 tablespoons honey

Preparation:

1. Mix both the ingredients in a small bowl.
2. The sauce is ready to be served.

Classic Soy and Vinegar Dipping Sauce for Dumplings

Yields about 1⅓ cup

Ingredients:

1 cup soy sauce

2 tablespoons rice vinegar

1 teaspoon sesame oil

1 or 2 green onions, diced finely

1 pinch or more of red hot chili flakes

¼ cup water

Preparation:

1. Whisk all the ingredients together in a small bowl.
2. Let the sauce rest at least 30 minutes before serving, so the flavors are well blended.
3. Store in an airtight container in the refrigerator.

Classic Plum Sauce

Yields about 6 cups

Ingredients:

12 cups fresh ripe dark skin plums, pitted

1½ cup onion, diced

1½ teaspoon fresh ginger, grated

2 cloves garlic, minced

1½ cup white sugar

¾ cup rice vinegar

1½ teaspoon dry coriander

1 teaspoon salt

2 pinches ground clove

2 pinches or more of red hot chili flakes

1½ cup water

Preparation:

1. In a large saucepan, add the plums, onions, garlic, ginger, and water. Bring to a boil on medium-high heat.
2. Reduce the heat to medium-low, cover and let the plums simmer for 30-45 minutes, or until the plums are very tender. Remove from heat.
3. Using a hand-held blender, reduce the plum mixture to a purée.

4. Add the vinegar, sugar and remaining spices. Stir to combine well. Bring to a boil on medium-high heat. Reduce the heat to medium-low and let the sauce simmer for about 60 minutes, until it thickens.
5. To can the plum sauce, used canning jars like Mason jars that will have been boiled first. Let the jars sit in a boiling water bath for about thirty minutes.
6. Store in a cool and dark place.

Quick and Easy Orange Dipping Sauce

Yields about 1¾ cup

Ingredients:
1 cup Thai sweet chili sauce

½ cup orange juice

1 tablespoon hot sauce like Sriracha (or more if you like it spicier)

1 teaspoon fresh ginger, grated

1 tablespoon orange marmalade

2 tablespoons rice vinegar

3 tablespoons grape seed oil

1 teaspoon white sugar

Preparation:
1. Place the ingredients in a food processor, except the grape seed oil. Pulse until you have smooth sauce.
2. As the food processor is working, gradually and slowly add the grape seed oil in a thin stream. It will emulsify the sauce.
3. Store unused sauce in the refrigerator.

Sweet and Sour Dipping Sauce

Yields about 1½ cup

Ingredients:
½ cup brown sugar

5 tablespoons rice vinegar

2 tablespoons tomato paste

2 tablespoons soy sauce

1 cup pineapple juice

1 teaspoon ginger paste

¼ teaspoon salt

1 tablespoon cornstarch

2 tablespoons water

Preparation:
1. Place the ingredients in a saucepan except the water and cornstarch. Bring to a boil on medium-high heat. Stir until the sugar is completely dissolved.
2. Bring the heat down to medium-low. Mix the water and cornstarch and add the paste to the saucepan. Whisk the sauce until it thickens, about 1 minute.
3. Serve warm or cold.
4. Store unused sauce in the refrigerator.

Sweet and Hot Dipping Sauce

Yields about 1 ¼ cup

Ingredients:

½ cup pineapple, diced

1 green onion

1 teaspoon ginger, grated

¼ cup rice vinegar

1 tablespoon Sriracha hot sauce

½ teaspoon brown sugar

½ cup water

3 tablespoons extra light olive oil

Preparation:

1. Heat 3 tablespoons olive oil in skillet, add green onion and sauté for a minute.
2. Add pineapple and sugar. Continue to stir until caramelization begins to form.
3. Add remaining ingredients, and bring to a boil.
4. Simmer sauce on low for 5 minutes, remove from heat and allow to cool down.
5. Using hand immersion blender, blend sauce until smooth.

Hot Chili Sauce

Yields about
Yields about 1 cup

Ingredients:

¾ cup rice wine vinegar

¼ cup sugar

1 teaspoon salt

4 tablespoons hot sauce like Sriracha

1 tablespoon tomato paste

½ teaspoon corn starch

Preparation:

1. Combine ingredients in blender, mix until smooth.

Honey Ginger Sauce

Yields about ⅔ cup

Ingredients:

½ cup pure honey

2 tablespoons sesame seeds

1 tablespoon ginger, grated

½ teaspoon salt

Preparation:

Combine ingredients and refrigerate for an hour before serving.

Caramel Dipping Sauce for Turon

Yields about 1 ½ cup

Ingredients:

1 12 oz can coconut milk

1 tablespoon butter

¾ cup brown sugar

Preparation:

1. Melt butter in skillet over medium heat, add sugar, and mix until caramelization begins.
2. Slowly add coconut milk while continuing to mix, bring to a boil, reduce heat and continue to mix until sauce is thick enough to coat a spoon.

Bonus Recipes

We hope that you enjoyed preparing and savoring the traditional egg rolls, spring rolls, dumpling and dim sum recipes. Here are five classic Asian appetizer recipes.

Shrimp Toasts

Serves: 20
Preparation time: 15 minutes
Cooking time: 40 minutes

Ingredients:

5 white sandwich bread slices

½ pound shrimp, shelled and deveined

1½ cup napa cabbage, shredded

½ tomato, finely chopped

2 green onions, finely chopped

1 teaspoon fresh ginger, grated

1 tablespoon fresh coriander

1 tablespoon sesame oil

1 teaspoon rice wine vinegar or dry sherry

1 egg, beaten

Salt and pepper

2 teaspoons cornstarch

4 cups vegetable oil or more for frying

Preparation:
1. Preheat the oven to 225°F/116°C and thaw the shrimp if they are frozen.
2. Remove the crusts from the bread and cut each to for 4 triangles.
3. Completely dry the bread by baking them for 10-15 minutes at 225°F/116°C, or until the bread is dry.
4. Place the oil in a saucepan and warm on medium-high heat.
5. In the meanwhile, place the remaining ingredients in the food processor. Pulse until you get a thick chunky paste.
6. Take the bread out of the oven and let the toasts cool.
7. Spoon the mixture evenly on top of each toast.
8. In batches, add bread pieces into the hot oil. Place the toasts with a slotted spoon, shrimp mixture face down. Fry for about 1 minute, until golden brown. Turn the toasts over and fry for another minute, until golden brown.
9. Remove the toasts and drain on paper towels.
10. You can also bake these toasts, if you do not like to deep fry. To do so, heat the oven to 375°F/191°C and bake the toasts for 15 minutes, until golden brown.
11. Serve while still hot.

Crispy Fried Wontons

Servings: 10
Preparation time: 10 minutes
Cooking time: 40 minutes

Ingredients:

¾ pound pork, ground

8 canned, water chestnuts

¼ cup green onions, finely chopped

1 tablespoon soya sauce

1 teaspoon cornstarch

½ teaspoon salt

½ teaspoon ginger, grated

1 packet wonton skin

Oil, for frying

Preparation:

1. In a mixing bowl, combine all the ingredients (except wonton skins and oil) to make a fine mixture. Mix well to ensure that all the ingredients are spread properly.
2. Heat the oil on a medium heat in a saucepan. You can also use a deep fryer.
3. Take a wonton skin, and lay it flat on a surface.
4. At its center, place ¼ to ½ teaspoon of the mixture.

5. Fold the wonton skin into half, covering the mixture.
6. Seal the wontons by slightly pressing down to fasten the dough around the pork mixture, leaving the edges unsealed.
7. Fry the wontons in small batches. Add the oil to a wok or large or a large frying pan and warm over medium-high heat.
8. Fry the wontons for around 2-3 minutes when the oil is hot. Remove with slotted spoon and place on paper towels to drain excess oil.
9. Serve hot or cold with a sweet and sour sauce.

Shrimp Balls

Serves: 35 balls
Preparation time: 40 minutes
Cooking time: 20 minutes

Ingredients:
1 pound medium shrimp, shelled and deveined
8 water chestnuts, chopped
½ green onion, finely chopped
½ fresh ginger, grated
2 teaspoons soy sauce
1 teaspoon rice wine vinegar
½ teaspoon white sugar
¼ teaspoon sesame oil
Fresh grounded black pepper
1 egg white
½ teaspoon cornstarch

Preparation:
1. Soak the shrimp in salted water for about 5 minutes.
2. Rinse them with cold water and dry using paper towels.
3. Mince both the shrimp and the chestnuts.
4. In a bowl, mix all the ingredients to form a fine mixture.

5. Make small balls of this mixture.
6. Heat the oil in a frying pan on a high heat. Slowly add the shrimp balls to the pan and make sure not to crowd the pan.
7. Fry the balls for 3-4 minutes or until they turn crisp and golden.
8. Remove the balls from the oil and drain on a tissue paper.
9. Serve the balls hot with a sweet and sour sauce or plum sauce.

Kon Tiki Bobo Meatballs

Serves: 6-8
Preparation time: 30 minutes
Cooking time: 10 minutes

Ingredients:

Meatball ingredients

1 pound ground pork

1 cup white bread crumbs

½ teaspoon ground ginger

¼ cup white sugar

1 garlic cloves, minced

Batter ingredients

1½ cup all-purpose flour

4 tablespoons white sugar

2 teaspoons baking soda

1 cup water

2 eggs

Salt and pepper

Oil for frying

Preparation:

1. In a mixing bowl, combine all the meatball ingredients. Season with salt and pepper.
2. Form meatballs of even sizes of about 1 inch in diameter. Set aside
3. To prepare the batter, mix the flour, sugar, baking soda. Season generously with salt and pepper. Pour the flour mix in a shallow dish.
4. In another shallow dish, mix together the eggs, and water.
5. Dip each meatball in the egg mixture and roll it in the flour mixture. Set aside on a plate.
6. Heat the oil for frying or you can also use a deep frying machine. Fry the meatballs in batches for 5 minutes. Place on a plate lined with paper towel to drain the excess fat.
7. Serve with cocktail toothpicks and a dipping sauce like sweet and sour or cherry sauce.

Tanguy BBQ Pork Short Ribs – Chinese style

An Asian twist to the traditional BBQ pork short ribs, the Asian spices and condiments compliment the succulent pork ribs.

Servings: 6-8
Preparation 30 minutes
Marinating time 8h00 or more
Cooking time: 1 hour

Ingredients:

4 pounds pork spareribs

Marinade ingredients

3 tablespoons light Soy sauce

3 tablespoons dark Soy sauce

1/3 cup hoisin Sauce

1 tablespoon ketchup

1 tablespoon rice vinegar

2 teaspoons brown Sugar

½ teaspoon Chinese five-spices

2 garlic cloves, finely chopped

¼ cup honey

½ cup boiling water

Preparation:
1. Mix together soya sauce, hoisin sauce, vinegar, ketchup, chopped garlic, and brown sugar.
2. Use this mixture to marinate the spare ribs and refrigerate it overnight.
3. Next day, pre-heat the oven to 350°F//177°F.
4. Mix honey with boiling water.
5. Take a shallow roasting pan and add half an inch of water to it.
6. Place this pan at the bottom of the oven.
7. Now place the marinated rib directly on a rack above the water.
8. Let the pork cook for 50 to 60 minutes.
9. During the roasting process, brush the ribs with the honey water a few times.
10. Remove from the oven and let it cool before serving.

CONCLUSION

Thank you again for purchasing my book. I hope you enjoyed the recipes and will prepare many from it. Asian appetizers, be it dumpling, egg rolls or spring rolls, are just amazing, simple food you can make and enjoy at home with friends and family. They are an important part of Asian cuisine. The flavors and techniques are very old ones, developed over centuries. A lot of recipes have stayed in families, passing from generation to generation.

Once you begin whipping up these delicious egg rolls, spring rolls and dumplings at home, it's going to be hard to stop. The beautiful fresh, flavors, colors and textures are a far cry from frozen or takeout, and the clean, simplicity the at-home chef can achieve is quite impressive. You will master the art of making these pockets full of joy in no time!

Although the recipes do call for frying, you can feel good about the fact that you are using all sorts of lovely veggies and proteins that are packed full of nutrients. Whether you are catering to vegetarians, spice lovers, carnivores or a mixed crowd, the recipes provided are sure to provide you with enough choices to please any palate.

Tweak and experiment once you feel comfortable and enjoy your bites of genius deliciousness at home.

Bon appétit!

ABOUT THE AUTHOR

Sarah Spencer, who lives in Canada with her husband and two children, describes herself as an avid foodie who prefers watching the Food Network over a hockey game or NCIS! She is a passionate cook who dedicates all her time between creating new recipes, writing cookbooks, and her family, though not necessarily in that order!

Sarah has had two major influences in her life regarding cooking, her Grandmother and Mama Li.

She was introduced to cooking at an early age by her Grandmother who thought cooking for your loved ones was the single most important thing in life. Not only that, but she was the World's Best Cook in the eyes of all those lucky enough to taste her well-kept secret recipes. Over the years, she conveyed her knowledge and appreciation of food to Sarah.

Sarah moved to Philadelphia when her father was transferred there when Sarah was a young teenager. She became close friends with a girl named Jade, whose parents owned a Chinese take-out restaurant. This is when Sarah met her second biggest influence,

Mama Li. Mama Li was Jade's mother and a professional cook in her own restaurant. Sarah would spend many hours in the restaurant as a helper to Mama Li. Her first job was in the restaurant. Mama Li showed Sarah all about cooking Asian food, knife handling, and mixing just the right amount of spices. Sarah became an excellent Asian cook, especially in Chinese and Thai food.

Along the way, Sarah developed her own style in the kitchen. She loves to try new flavors and mix up ingredients in new and innovative ways. She is also very sensitive to her son's allergy to gluten and has been cooking gluten-free and paleo recipes for quite some time.

Shown below are some of her other books. They are available on Amazon.

MORE
FREEZER MEALS
FOR THE
SLOW COOKER
QUICK AND EASY RECIPES FOR BUSY PEOPLE
SARAH SPENCER

Totally
Thai
Classic Thai Recipes to Make at Home
SARAH SPENCER

Thanksgiving
Feast Cookbook
The Very Best Classic and
New Recipes
Sarah Spencer

CHRISTMAS
FEAST COOKBOOK
The Very Best Classic and
New Recipes
SARAH SPENCER

DELICIOUS
200-CALORIE
DESSERT
RECIPES
Perfect for Your Sweet Tooth
and Waistline!
SARAH SPENCER

SIMPLE
PALEO
SALAD
COOKBOOK
50 QUICK & EASY
GLUTEN-FREE SALAD RECIPES
FEEL ENERGIZED, LOSE WEIGHT
AND LOOK HEALTHY
SARAH SPENCER

Gluten Free
TODAY
36 QUICK & EASY LUNCH
AND SNACK RECIPES
SARAH SPENCER

APPENDIX

Cooking Conversion Charts

1. Volumes

US Fluid Oz.	US	US Dry Oz.	Metric Liquid ml
¼ oz.	2 tsp.	1 oz.	10 ml.
½ oz.	1 tbsp.	2 oz.	15 ml.
1 oz.	2 tbsp.	3 oz.	30 ml.
2 oz.	¼ cup	3½ oz.	60 ml.
4 oz.	½ cup	4 oz.	125 ml.
6 oz.	¾ cup	6 oz.	175 ml.
8 oz.	1 cup	8 oz.	250 ml.

Tsp.= teaspoon - tbsp.= tablespoon – oz.= ounce – ml.= millimeter

2. Oven Temperatures

Celsius (°C)	Fahrenheit (°F)*
90	220
110	225
120	250
140	275
150	300
160	325
180	350
190	375
200	400
215	425
230	450
250	475
260	500

*Rounded numbers

Printed in Great Britain
by Amazon.co.uk, Ltd.,
Marston Gate.